Temping

The Insider's Guide

Richard M. Rogers

MACMILLAN • USA

Macmillan General Reference
A Simon & Schuster Macmillan Company
1633 Broadway
New York, NY 10019-6785

An Arco Book

Manufactured in the United States of America

10 9 8 7 6 5 4 3 2 1

Library of Congress Cataloging-in-Publication Data 96-086620

ISBN: 0-02-861060-1

Book design by A&D Howell

To My Mother

Table of Contents

Acknowledgments

Many people, inside and outside the temporary employment industry, contributed to the creation of this book. I would not have been able to do it without them. My thanks:

To the temporary workers, both those who agreed to be interviewed for this book and those many workers who I've met through the years and whose experiences have in some way formed the inspiration and the basis for this book. My special thanks go to Arthur, Becky, Brian, Carl, Christina, Evelyn, Helen, Jack, Jamie, Laura, Paul, Sally, and Sarah.

To Bruce Steinberg of the National Association of Temporary and Staffing Services for his support and enthusiasm from the moment I called him, and for putting me in touch with temporary help services across the country. And for reading a draft of this book, my thanks.

To the folks at the temporary help services who took the time to fill out questionnaires, field numerous follow-up questions, and scoured their companies for temporary workers to be interviewed: Yvette Folk, a friend and personnel counselor at Winston Staffing Services, Inc.; Gretchen Kreske of Manpower, Inc.; Bryce Arrowood of LawCorps® Legal Staffing Services; Bobby Riggins of Talent Tree Staffing Services, Inc.; Sarah J. Marks of The Executive Source; Derek Kipp of Special Counsel International; Faye Sherwood and Cheryl Ann Van Beek of

Norrell Corporation; Corina Berenberg and Robert A. Funk of Express Personnel Services; Lorren Strong of CompHealth/Kron; David Marth of DayStar® Temporary Services, Inc.; and Adrienne Plotch of The Olsten Corporation.

To Tom Rodenhauser of Kennedy Publications who spent so much time on the phone with me shedding light on the ins and outs of interim executive temping.

To father and son Bert Holtje and James Holtje. James for suggesting that a book like this may be needed; Bert for making sure it got to the right publisher.

And last, but certainly not least, to my girlfriend and fellow writer, Karen Kingsbury, who not only made my life easier during the course of the writing of this book, but also devoted her time and considerable skill to reading a draft of the book and whose suggestions have, no doubt, improved it.

Introduction

· ·

Imagine a future where the largest and most powerful corporations are temporary help service companies. All work is assigned through these agencies. No one works a permanent full-time job in the way we understand it today.

This idea is at once intriguing and perhaps a little frightening. For the vast majority of us, it will probably never come to that. But the idea may not be as far-fetched as it sounds. For some 8 million American workers who are employed as temporaries, either voluntarily or due to the inability to find a permanent job, that future is already here. For millions more it will no doubt come.

The fact is, the temporary help services industry has grown at a phenomenal rate in the past few years and is now among the fastest-growing service businesses in America. Manpower, Inc., the nation's largest of the more than 7,000 temporary help services, employs about 900,000 people. That makes it the biggest private employer in the U.S. Bigger than General Motors. Bigger than IBM. Nationwide, the use of temporary workers has almost doubled over the past decade and all indications are that the numbers of temporary workers will continue to rise.

It would be difficult, if not impossible, to find a single industry sector that did not employ temporary workers—advertising, telecommunications, manufacturing, and high-tech industries to name just a few. And in every industry more companies use temporary workers than ever before. In fact, 95% of U.S. companies today employ temporary workers in some capacity or other. Many companies factor in the use of temporary personnel as part of their normal operating budgets.

Nor do temporary workers occupy the lowest rungs of the corporate ladder anymore. In today's corporation, temps can be found in the mail room as well as the boardroom—and in every position in-between. Temporary workers do not just fill in for the vacationing secretary; they have become an integral and often crucial factor to the corporate bottom line.

Temporary workers have become, in a word, "respectable." Quite a few temps, even when offered full-time positions, opt to remain temporaries. There are opportunities in this field that just didn't exist a few years ago. These opportunities will increase as companies continue to downsize, become "lean and mean" as well as project-oriented, and seek out the highly skilled workers required in today's computer environment. Unfortunately, competition for the best and highest paid temporary positions will also become stiffer.

The temporary help environment is changing rapidly, as is the corporate environment it serves. Gone are the days when a person could just walk into a temporary help services company, take a couple of tests and walk out with an assignment. Because the focus has changed from temp worker as fill-in to temp worker as corporate team member, temporary help companies often seek the same qualities in their employees as corporations seek in their full-time staff. Temporary help services often provide specific training for specific client needs. Client companies themselves may request to interview a number of temps before deciding which one will fit their needs—a development unheard of just a year ago.

This book will help you keep pace with this changing environment and take advantage of the many opportunities opening up in this field.

The information this book contains should be useful whether you choose to temp, need to temp, or whether you are already temping. The chapters cover all aspects of temping, starting with some reasons why temping is so extensive and proceeding on to practical advice on how to select a temporary help service and how to work with that service to get the best paying assignments. Also included is information on finding full-time work through temping, how to make a career of temping, and the rapidly expanding area of high-end temping—doctors, lawyers, and senior executives.

My own experience in this field has been quite extensive. I have earned a living through temping on and off for ten years and have temped for many corporations, large and small, in two major metropolitan areas. I have been offered two full-time positions through temping, one of which I took. I have seen a lot of changes through the years and have developed some thoughts about where this industry is going. I will be sharing these thoughts with you during the course of this book. You also will get to know a number of other temps and hear how they have turned their temping experiences into successful ones. You will benefit from literally hundreds of years of temping experience.

You also will hear directly from temporary help service personnel and learn from them the inside information about what to expect at an interview, how to develop a winning relationship with your coordinator, and what areas are expected to be the hottest in the coming years. Equally important, you'll learn about how to deal with the client company and what you need to do to build up a core group of client companies that keep calling you back. The client companies pay the bills, after all, and what you do there is important to your success as a temporary worker.

My own temping experience has essentially been a positive one. But, as with every industry, there is a downside along with the upside. This book will explore both. It is my hope that this book will equip you with all the essential facts, help you have a successful temping experience, and if your future should lie in temping, to be better prepared for it.

America's Changing Workscape

Y ou are now, or may become, a member of one of the fastest growing industry sectors in America today. You are a temp. Today, temporary workers can be found in almost all industries and professions from
the mailroom to the boardroom, from the hospital gift shop to the
operating room, from the legal word-processing office to the court-
room, and everywhere in between. The rise in temporary employment
in the past two decades has been nothing short of phenomenal. Consider these facts:

- Just over ten years ago, about 165,000 people were employed each
  day in a temporary capacity. By 1995 that number had grown to
  more than 2.2 million.

- Since 1970, the temporary help industry has expanded at a
  double-digit annual rate, making it one of the fastest growing
  service industries in America.

- Since 1991, one out of every six new jobs created has been a temp job.
- Currently, 1.78% of total non-agricultural employment is filled by a temporary employee.
- Ninety-five percent of American companies use temporary workers to supplement their full-time staffs.

Is this dramatic increase in temporary workers just a transitory condition in the workscape of America? Or does it signal a fundamental shift in the way we work that is likely to continue? Temporary agencies and industry experts predict that not only will this trend continue, it will accelerate.

Bobby Riggins, a director of marketing for Talent Tree Staffing Services, a national temporary help company says:

> The use of temporary workers is now part of a solid human resource strategy and is rooted in organizational profitability, so it is doubtful that this will diminish in the future. Companies are now starting to include the use of contingent staffing in their strategic plans and fully integrating contingent staffing into their overall business planning.

This is good news if you need to seek employment through a temporary help company. There are thousands of job opportunities: opportunities that didn't exist in the past, opportunities that will pay the bills in-between jobs, and opportunities that may provide you with the means of fulfilling your personal goals.

Of course, temping hasn't always been like this. Before the explosion of companies turning to temporary workers, temps were used exclusively to fill in for permanent employees who were on vacation or sick leave. Although temps still fill these slots, that image has gone the way of the rotary phone and manual typewriter. Today's new temp is a respected person with skills and aptitude. He or she is involved in crucial projects, often long-term, and has gained an equal place alongside his or her permanent counterparts in the workforce. As a group, temps are the most productive members of the workforce, according to a study by the National Association of Temporary and Staffing Services.

How did this change from temp as fill-in to temp as strategic worker come about? The answer is rooted in the change of the American corporation itself. We will explore the reasons why 95 percent of American corporations have made the decision to incorporate temporary workers into their overall strategy later in this chapter. I think you will agree with the experts that temping is here to stay.

Temping: The Insider's Guide will show you what it means to be a temp, how to choose the service that's best for you, and most important of all, how to make the best out of your temping experience.

You will meet people who have become today's new temps and gain an inside view on the temping industry. If you decide (or are forced) to join the ever-increasing temporary workforce, their experiences, advice, and tips will help make your transition toward successful temping easier.

The Corporate Quandary

It's no secret that corporations have been undergoing drastic changes in the past two decades. News of mergers, acquisitions, downsizings (also called "rightsizing") assail us daily in the media. Corporations have sought to "cut out the fat" to stay competitive on a global scale. While this has, unfortunately, meant the loss of millions of traditional full-time jobs, it has opened up a new market for the temporary worker.

At the same time, companies have had to contend with a host of new government rules and regulations, many of which have benefitted the temporary employment industry. For example, a company with 50 employees falls under the provisions of the Family and Medical Leave Act, which allows an employee a leave of absence for up to twelve unpaid weeks to care for a new baby or to take care of a sick family member. Who is going to fill in for that permanent employee? A temporary worker.

Other government regulations often make the hiring of new full-time employees a matter of so much red tape that small companies often find it prohibitive to increase the level of their permanent staffs beyond the bare minimum necessary. Companies with just fifteen employees become subject to the Civil Rights Act and the Americans with Disabilities Act. When a company reaches twenty employees, it becomes subject to the Age Discrimination Act. At 100 employees, the Worker Adjustment and Retraining Notification ("Plant Closing") Act takes effect. While no one would dispute the ethical issues surrounding compliance to any of these regulations, the fact is that a small employer finds the strategic use of temporary employees more cost-effective and hassle free.

In general, companies have found that the use of temps is a cost-effective and efficient means of keeping productivity up while keeping overhead down. Here's why:

Pay Only for What You Need: Hiring a temporary worker means that the company incurs no cost for absenteeism. The company only pays for the actual hours a temporary employee works.

Staff for the Valleys: Every industry and every company within an industry experiences ups and downs in their production cycle during the course of a year. Companies used to staff for the peak periods year-round.

"Now they are staffing for the valleys," says Gretchen Kreske, information specialist for Manpower, Inc., the nation's largest temporary help service. "When corporations have production peaks, they can add the extra, supplemental staff they need for that time. It's a strategic way to stay competitive."

This "flex force" helps companies stay lean and mean, a necessity in today's global economy.

Keeping Morale Intact: The recent downsizings, with their resulting lay-offs, have had a negative impact on remaining full-time staff. Employees have become, understandably, worried about job security. They have also been called upon to pick up the slack by working longer hours. Both of these factors contribute to low employee morale. Companies don't want to hire new full-time employees only to have to fire them again. The use of temporary employees can help pick up the slack while testing the viability of a possible full-time position—and keep employee morale high.

Concentrate on Core Business: Companies have realized that they have a core business that is supported by auxiliary staff. By turning over auxiliary staffing needs to other companies, such as a temporary service, companies can concentrate on the most productive and profitable areas of their business.

Saving at the Fringes: Fringe benefits can be expensive. The U.S. Chamber of Commerce notes that "hidden" costs, such as mandatory taxes and insurance, company paid benefits, etc., can add up to 38 percent to the salary of each full-time employee. This has created a disincentive to hire full-time workers in favor of temporary workers. Many companies now only hire additional full-time staff when their own employees working overtime and a supplemental temporary staff still can't get the job done.

Saving on Recruiting: Companies also save on the costs involved in recruiting, testing, training, and turnover. According to the National Association of Temporary and Staffing Services, recruiting and hiring a full-time employee can add 5 to 20 percent to the cost of an employee. By letting a temporary service, in effect, do the recruitment and hiring, a corporation saves time and money. In fact, when it comes to hiring additional full-time employees, many companies find that testing them out first as temporary workers is the most efficient way to go.

If it was just a matter of watching out for the bottom line, corporations would have reason enough to justify the extensive use of temporary workers, but there is another, perhaps even more important reason why there has been such a dramatic increase in the use of temps over the past two decades and why temps will continue to find opportunities in the years to come: the increase of office automation and personal computers.

The Technology Dilemma

Corporations have poured $1 trillion into high-tech gadgetry of all types in the hope of making their companies run more efficiently and more profitably. But what's the point of having the fastest computers or computer applications that can do everything but cook breakfast in the morning if you can't find qualified personnel to use them?

There's a term in computer jargon called "GIGO." It means garbage in, garbage out. Corporations soon found that rather than making life easier, technology created its own demands and requirements. Trained personnel were needed and they were not so easily found. Rather than get the model of efficiency corporations expected, they got garbage in many cases. Finding trained personnel is difficult. The available labor pool is not supplying it and is responding slowly. That is reflected in a U.S. Department of Labor report that noted obsolete skills were responsible for 85 percent of unemployment in the last recession.

The Occupational Outlook Handbook published by the Department of Labor reports there has been a chronic shortage of skilled clerical and technical help available in this country since 1974. The gap between the needs of technology and the people who know how to use it is expected to widen. The result has been that employers are finding it more and more difficult to locate the highly skilled employees they need and the amount of time it takes to find these employees is far too long. Once found, new hirees often require expensive training. In some cases, positions can no longer be filled in the traditional sense at all. Where do corporations find the skilled people they need?

Temporary help service companies, traditionally strong in the office/clerical field, have been quick to respond to the rapidly changing demands of today's technology. There is no question these conditions have been one of the prime factors in the exponential growth of the temporary services industry. Business has, therefore, relied heavily on these companies to supply them with people capable of working on personal computers and who are well trained in all the latest software packages. Temporary help services are in the forefront in training and cross-training people on all popular software applications and in responding to their clients' technological needs. In some cases, temporary help companies train temps on a specific client application, relieving the client of the expense of both hiring and training their own full-time employees. Some temporary help service companies even train full-time employees on the latest software packages as a service to their clients. The marriage between the temporary help service industry and the corporate sector has proven to be an extremely satisfying one for both parties. A divorce any time soon is unlikely.

A New Social Perspective

The corporate side is not the only one defining the new workscape. Many of us have begun to look at the traditional employer-employee relationship through different-colored glasses. Here are some of the factors that have changed the way we look at work:

A New Need for Flexibility: Public opinion surveys indicate employees also want a change toward a more flexible work style, balancing priorities between work and home. A national poll conducted in 1993 by the Gallup Organization, Inc. for Accountants on Call found that 66 percent of employed adults—regardless of gender, education, or occupation—would prefer to work ten hours a day, four days a week, so that they could have three days off. Similarly, in a study conducted a year later by the Families and Work Institute, New York, entitled "The National Study of the Changing Workforce," it was reported that 33 percent of employees would be willing to exchange salary and other benefits for the opportunity of taking time off for parenting.

Clearly, the American worker has voiced a strong desire for flex-time working arrangements. Just as clearly, many of us have turned to temporary employment as the means to satisfy our flex-time requirements. Needless to say, the temporary industry has welcomed, with open arms, those people with personal needs.

A More Mobile Workforce: Our mobility has also played a role in our employment choices. *American Demographics* reports that about one in seven people in the United States annually relocate to another city. Seeking work through a temporary employment service may be the best avenue for many of these people as they carry their portable skills from city to city and town to town.

The Age Factor: People are living longer and many retirees are not content with just staying at home barely making ends meet on a fixed income. They also want to feel productive, according to a poll conducted by the American Association of Retired Persons. The poll showed that three out of four Americans, aged 55-64, would rather work than retire. But many retired people say they don't want the rigors and responsibilities of full-time employment, and many have found the income and the freedom they need through temporary work.

It All Adds Up

No matter how you look at it—from the corporate side or from the social side—we have entered an era where the employer-employee relationship has been redefined. For some 2.2 million of us, the new definition includes seeking employment and fulfillment through temporary work. Indeed, becoming a temporary worker has become a viable employment alternative for all kinds of people. Perhaps you will be one of them.

At the rate the temporary worker industry is growing, more than 500,000 people will join the ranks of the temporary worker force in the next few years. According to figures by the Bureau of Labor Statistics and the National Association of Temporary and Staffing Services, temporary workers, as a percentage of total employment, will grow to 3 percent—an 88 percent increase—by the year 2000. Some predict temporary employees will make up an even larger percentage of the total workforce shortly after the turn of the century.

If you are already working as a temp or will be, either voluntarily or involuntarily, you have the advantage of coming into the industry at a time when corporations view you as an integral part of their structure. Additionally, you can be encouraged by the fact that temping is here to stay and is a viable means of making an income in both good economic times and bad.

In good economic times, temporary workers can expect their salaries to rise because the demand for skilled labor is greater than the supply. During the bad times, when the labor supply is greater than the demand, temp workers have an advantage over those seeking full-time work because there is always a need for fill-in, short-term positions and long-term, project-oriented work, and the temporary industry is adept at placing its employees. So adept, in fact, that a temporary company can fill a position in 24 hours, compared to the six weeks it takes for a traditional employment service to fill a position.

According to the U.S. Chamber of Commerce, 75 percent of U.S. companies plan for the use of temporary help, and 95 percent use temporary help annually. Temping has become an acceptable way to earn a salary. As a temp, you can expect to earn as much as, and sometimes more than, your full-time peers. The idea that a person is "just a temp" is extinct. Today, you are an accepted part of a corporation's bottom line.

On the downside, with so many workers expected to enter the temporary market, this already competitive field will become even more so. As a temporary worker, you will have to market yourself aggressively, keep up with rapid changes in technology, and learn as much as you can about how the industry works to get the best jobs. We will cover all of these subjects thoroughly in this book.

In the next chapter we will define some general industry terms and discuss the pluses and minuses of temping. After that, we will look specifically into the reasons why people temp and the type of people who do. That will be followed by a closer look at the relationship between the temporary help company and the client company and how you can navigate between the two to make your temping experience a success.

Welcome to the world of temporary employment. Good luck.

Temping— What Is It?

Through my years as a temp, I've met a lot of individuals who have temped for many different reasons. It's safe to say that there are as many reasons for temping as there are people who temp. In general, people choose temporary work for two reasons:

Temping as a Means to an End: For the vast majority of temps, temping is a means to something else, such as providing an income between jobs, finding a job, or pursuing a wide variety of creative, personal, or business endeavors. For example, Jack, an entrepreneur in his mid-fifties, started doing temporary work about four years ago so he could pursue a career as an independent consultant. He sees something in temping that is generally felt but rarely articulated: "Temping is the thing that provides one with hope for 'the other' occupation while keeping a roof over one's head."

Jack puts it well; temping is about hope. I've met many of these people along the way, and I've seen how they become successful at temping: They apply that same energy to their temping careers as they do to their primary goals.

Temping as an End in Itself: As a means to an end, temping can be, and is, a rewarding experience. There was a time in the not too distant past that just about everyone who temped had a reason for doing so. But, increasingly, temping has become an end in itself. Almost 40 percent of temporary workers, in fact, want to remain a temporary employee indefinitely according to a survey of temporary workers conducted by the National Association of Temporary and Staffing Services. This figure indicates that these "career temps" have found that temping provides them with, at the very least, the income they need and the job satisfaction we all seek. They also might be considered the best of the industry, and the way they have become successful may be worth emulating. It is worth reading chapter 10, which is devoted to career temping, even if you have no intention of making it a career.

Temping Definitions

Whether you see temping as a means to an end or as an end in itself, the term *temporary employee* has a certain standard definition.

All Temps are Employees of the Temporary Employment Service: Confusion among temporary workers about who is the actual employer is fairly common in the temporary industry. Surveys by the National Association of Temporary and Staffing Services, for example, show that one third of temps think they are employed by the company they are assigned to. Considering that most of your contact will be with a client company, it can be easy to forget who employs you. However, your success at temping could be hindered if you forget this important fact. Assignments and client companies come and go; your ongoing relationship must be with the service. Always keep in mind who your employer is and this will give you the right perspective.

All Temps Work for a Specified Period of Time: This specified period of time, called the assignment length, can run from a day to a year, or longer. The time is usually discussed before the assignment starts, but, in actuality, there are no hard and fast rules when it comes to length of assignments. Assignments that were originally scheduled for three weeks could go on for months; conversely, assignments that were originally billed as long-term could end after a day. However, temps are doing much more than they used to do and the average length of an assignment has increased considerably. It's not unusual in today's market to find assignments that last six months or more.

And finally, no matter how long or short a temporary assignment lasts, a temporary job is just that—temporary. Sooner or later, the assignment will end and a new one will begin.

The Temp Image

Rightly or wrongly, we are all concerned with our image and what we do for a living plays an important part in how we view ourselves. Perhaps you've heard that temporary employees do not enjoy a good image or are considered something less than capable. There have been considerable changes in America's workscape over the past two decades. In the previous chapter we had a look at some of the more important ones. We've seen how many of these changes have made a positive impact on the temporary industry. With the increased use of temps, longer assignments, and the entry of doctors, lawyers, and other professionals into the temporary worker sector, the image of a temp has also undergone some radical changes.

The old image of the temp, embodied so smartly in the Kelly Girl advertisements as the fill-in secretary called to replace a sick worker, is no longer valid. Kelly Girl—now prefers to be referred to as Kelly Services, Inc. with hundreds of jobs in various categories. Like the Kelly image change, today's temporary worker is an entirely different species. Temps are now an integral and crucial part of a corporate budget. Temps can be found in offices, in executive suites, in hospitals and nursing homes, on the assembly line, and on the airport runway. It would be difficult to find a company that did not, at some point, use temporary employees. There's no doubt that temps have become a staple of modern business practice.

With this new image should come a feeling of self-respect. Whatever your reasons for choosing this line of work, you should never think of yourself as "just a temp." You are a temporary employee. Each day you fill any one of more than 100 different positions, ranging from office/clerical to industrial to medical to technical/professional. You are a crucial and essential element to the bottom line of the company you help.

But what does that mean to you and what benefits can you derive from these facts? First, and most important, it means that companies eagerly hire temporary employees. Your chances of finding work when and where you want it have increased dramatically.

Second, it means your contribution to the workplace will be treated with respect and recognition, and you will receive a fair rate of compensation. Temporary workers now enjoy salaries that are competitive with, and often greater than, their permanently employed counterparts.

Image and rate of compensation are definitely two of the pluses of being a temporary worker. Like any industry, the temporary help services field has its own positives and negatives. But since this is a rather unique industry, these may not be so readily apparent. Let's take a closer look at temping's pluses and minuses to help you determine if temping is right for you.

Temping—The Pluses

Freedom and Flexibility: The biggest plus in becoming a temporary worker is the flexibility and choice it offers you. As a temp, you are free to accept or refuse any assignment. Of course, once you accept an assignment you are expected to complete it. This freedom to choose allows you to tailor a work schedule to meet your needs. It can translate in different ways to different people. If you want to travel or just take time off to do other personal things, temping enables you to do that. Temporary help jobs are available all over the world, including Canada, Europe, South America, Australia, and Africa. For free spirits, creative people, students, retirees, and moonlighters, the flexibility temping offers can be an ideal situation. I know one temp, for example, who temps in New York City for six months and in Paris for the other six months. How's that for freedom?

The Ability to Generate Income Quickly: There is probably no other industry sector that allows you to make money as quickly as the temporary industry. Temporary help service companies take only about 24 hours to fill a position once they get a call from a client company. An employer takes from six to eight weeks to fill a permanent job from the time they first find out about an opening. That means, of course, that the chances of you making money are increased considerably.

Although one of the biggest pluses in working temporarily is the ability to generate income quickly, you should not expect to get an assignment immediately if you haven't already established a relationship with a temporary service. For one, the service has to check your references before they send you out on an assignment. Other factors that enter into the picture include your flexibility, test scores, area of expertise, and your geographic location. Just like any other economic situation, it comes down to a matter of supply and demand.

In later chapters, we'll check out ways to speed up this process and also how to market yourself. But, for now, keep in mind that at first you may not always be able to make money as fast as you would like. This means you will have to do a certain amount of planning. If you are unemployed, for example, you should not wait until your Unemployment Insurance benefits are about to run out. Sign up with a service immediately.

Variety: Another big plus is the variety temping offers. You can work in the telecommunications industry one week, advertising the next, and hospitality the third. Every industry segment is represented. Depending on your experience and skill, you can work in any of more than 100 different positions filled by temporaries each day. Temporary workers can be placed in just about any type of position. This variety and change is ideal for people who are looking to change careers, for students and recent grads who want to get a feel for a number of different industries, for people who like facing new challenges and situations, and for retirees who enjoy a change of pace.

Getting the Inside Scoop: Temping gives you the opportunity to look for something else to do with your life. Christina began temping after she quit her long-time job as a journalist in Palm Springs, California, and moved back to her hometown of Sacramento. "I didn't really want to go back into journalism but I didn't know how to make any money until a friend told me about temping. It was great," says Christina.

She found that temping gave her a perspective on a company that she would not get any other way. "It gave me the opportunity to look into different organizations from very small to large corporations and to kind of get a feeling for how they worked and how they were run and whether I would even be interested in working in that organization. I've worked in some places where the office politics were so obvious I would never want to work there. Then I've also been in places where everyone's mellow. There's a real sense of teamwork and respect. And whether you're a temp or a full-time employee, everybody is afforded mutual respect as a worker and employee. And, of course, that's the kind of organization I would like to work at."

Not only did Christina find this inside look into a company advantageous, she also found that temping opened doors that would otherwise be closed. "Once you're working as a temp, you have easier access to what jobs are open and are able to explore any possibilities for promotions and things like that." Christina advises, "Talk to the employees and see if the company promotes from within or if it always hires from the outside. I think [temping] is a good opportunity to explore the options that are available in the work area where you're located, without having to make a commitment."

A Load of Experience: When it comes to gaining on-the-job experience, temping is like stepping into a time warp. You can gain more experience faster through temping than, perhaps, any other way. Sarah, who has been temping on and off for 20 years has found it an incredible learning experience. "Working in different environments and different situations makes you more flexible. In a year of temping you can get up to five years of actual experience," says Sarah, "because you have exposure to so many different situations that you would never get in a place where you come in and work at the same job everyday. Instead of working for one person in a year, you may work for 30, facing the same job in many different ways, depending on the person you work for."

Temping—The Minuses

Sometimes what's a plus for some is a minus for others. While flexibility and change are most often cited as being two of the most exciting features of temping, both have their minus side.

Flexibility, the Two-Edged Sword: While a service will make every attempt to provide you with a schedule that fits your needs, you, the temp, must ultimately be the one who is flexible. If you can only work from 1 to 5 p.m. on Mondays and Fridays, your chances of getting work will be severely hindered. If you turn down assignments too often, the service will stop calling you. Turning down one or two may be okay, but showing the service that you are consistently rigid would probably end your temping career before it starts.

The saying, "In order to get you have to give," holds true for your success as a temp. You have to prove your value and worth to the service before you make demands. There also will be times when your service will call you and ask you to take an assignment as a favor to them. Obviously, when you prove your flexibility, you will get flexibility in return. If your time constraints are such that it is impossible for you to be flexible, or otherwise cannot put in the time necessary to build a rapport with your service, then temping may not be for you.

Too Much of a Good Thing: It's fun and exciting to have variety and change but all this variety can produce a stress of its own. You cannot avoid the fact that you will have to prove yourself to the client company and its employees at each assignment. As a temp, you will experience the "first day jitters" regularly. Of course, if you are confident in your ability, that should be no problem. If you are the type of person who has difficulty facing new situations, temping may not be right for you.

No Career Path: While temping can get your foot in the door, it does not offer a career path. If you are interested in getting into the fast lane, looking for upward mobility, or are trying to find a mentor in a particular field, temping is probably not the best route to go.

No Job Security: Not that there's much job security anywhere these days, but temping would certainly rank at the bottom of the list if job security is your goal. There are no guarantees, no commitments, no written contracts. Jobs that are scheduled for three weeks may last a day. Conversely, jobs that were supposed to last a day may go on indefinitely. If you're looking for something absolutely certain, then temping would not be for you. Of course, as the saying goes, there's nothing certain but death and taxes.

Where Are the Fringe Benefits? While the income side of the equation is one of the temporary industry's strengths, the benefits side is not. Temporary workers do not get the company-paid benefits normally associated with full-time employment. For creative people, students and those in need of flexible hours, this is often an acceptable tradeoff. If you are temping for a second income, are a retiree on Medicare, have a spouse whose insurance plan covers you, or are otherwise covered by an individual health plan, this may not be a concern for you either. However, benefits are a legitimate concern for many temps.

As the industry has expanded, temporary help service companies have begun to address the needs of their employees in this area. Many companies now offer group health insurance plans; holiday, sick, and vacation pay; bonuses; life insurance; and retirement plans. Most of the offered benefits depend upon how many hours you work. We'll explore these benefits in more detail in a later chapter.

The Perennial Outsider: Since you are constantly changing worksites, you may not have the opportunity to get acquainted with co-workers or feel like part of a team. You may have to trade the personal nature of permanent employment for the freedom and flexibility of temporary employment. If you need to feel like you belong, or you get possessive, then temping can be very hard emotionally.

Successful Temp Check List

Now that you have some idea of the pluses and minuses of working as a temporary employee, it's important to ask yourself if you can be successful in this industry.

- Can you hit the ground running?
- Can you learn quickly?
- Can you adapt to different situations well?
- Do you enjoy challenges?
- Do you get excited about new situations and people?
- Do you have the ability to move on when necessary?
- Are you entrepreneurial?
- Can you take advantage of opportunities as they arise?
- Are you self-disciplined?
- Are you well organized?

- Are you punctual?
- Do you feel stifled by routine?
- Are you self-assured?
- Can you be flexible?
- Can you sell yourself?

If you've answered yes to some or all of these questions, then you can become a successful temporary worker. In the next chapter, we'll take a closer look at the types of people who most often temp and meet more of the temps who have been doing it successfully.

Temping— Who Does It and Why?

If you are already a temporary employee or will soon be entering the field, perhaps you'd like to know a little about your fellow temps.

The Temp Profile

Here's what a survey of temporary workers conducted by the National Association of Temporary and Staffing Services found:

- Half of all temporary workers are between 35 and 64 years of age.
- Temporary workers are predominantly female but the gender gap is closing quickly.
- Almost 75 percent have more than a high school education with five percent of all temporary workers earning advanced degrees.
- Over 80 percent are computer literate.

It is interesting to note that temporary workers, as a group, have the two qualities most in demand in today's corporate environment— education and computer literacy. Perhaps that's one of the reasons they are in such high demand.

The survey also found that there was a significant change in the reasons why people do temporary work from a similar survey conducted in 1989. The "average" temp now does it because he or she can't find a permanent job and has no other choice. That statistic shouldn't be surprising, considering the recent wave of lay-offs brought about by downsizing. Downsizings and corporate take-overs are on the rise once again, so, unfortunately, we can expect these trends to continue. Challenger Gray & Christmas, Inc., outplacement specialists, predicted in the January 8, 1996 edition of *Business Week* that corporate layoffs for 1996 would match the 1995 level of more than 400,000 people.

Still, about a third temp voluntarily because they like the flexibility it provides. Of the workers who become temps involuntarily, one third end up choosing temping as a lifestyle of choice.

If you happen to be in the majority and are looking for permanent employment, you should consider the fact that employers routinely hire temporary workers for full-time positions. According to a study conducted by the National Association of Temporary and Staffing Services, 38 percent of all temporary workers are offered a full-time job at the company or organization where they were on assignment. In fact, if you are looking for a job, temporary work may provide you with the best alternative to finding and getting a good position. All of the larger temporary staffing services offer official "temp-to-perm" opportunities but there are also many unofficial ways of getting full-time work through temping. We'll explore the official and unofficial ways later in this book.

As you will soon see, temping is a viable and acceptable means of earning an income. It can be used on a short-term basis to help get through a financial crisis, or on a long-term basis as a lifestyle choice. Temporary work can be tailored to fit almost anyone for any reason.

A survey can only give us a feel for the numbers, but not for the people behind them or the situations that lead them to temping. Let's take a look at some temps and some situations to find out why temping is useful. Perhaps you will see yourself or hear your story in one of the following anecdotes.

In-Between Jobs

Getting fired or laid-off has never been easy and it's certainly not easier today when the prospect of finding another job is difficult.

Perhaps the last thing you ever imagined being was a temp. You planned on working in a job long-term. But the days when a person can feel secure in a job until retirement are over. Your company has just downsized, merged, been bought, or some other event has occurred and your position has just been eliminated. Without doubt, this is a difficult time for you. Perhaps your spouse works and that will help, but, the fact is, your family most likely needs two incomes. There are bills to pay and your Unemployment Insurance benefits just won't cut it.

Let's face it, it's a tough job market out there and temping can be an excellent stop-gap measure to ensure some financial stability. In many cases, it can be a quick way to make money. Even if you have limited office or clerical skills, the temporary services industry offers many opportunities in many areas.

According to the National Association of Temporary and Staffing Services, 54 percent of temporaries temp because they are in-between jobs and the money they earn helps make ends meet.

If you are currently collecting Unemployment Insurance, it can do no harm (and will no doubt do some good) to get yourself to a temporary staffing service and sign up. If your Unemployment Insurance has run out, then run, don't walk, to a temporary staffing service. But read the rest of this book first to find out how you can best market your skills and maximize your earning potential in this increasingly competitive field.

You will also be able to extend the time period over which you can receive unemployment benefits by working as a temp. On the weeks that you work, your Unemployment Insurance for that week will be added to the end of your regular unemployment term. For more information about how working as a temporary employee affects your Unemployment Insurance benefits, you should contact your local Unemployment Insurance office.

Sometimes finding a way to make money after the loss of a job is only part of your dilemma. In addition to financial worries, there is also the psychological and social impact the loss of a job creates. The loss of a job in many cases also means the loss of self-esteem. You might feel bitter, depressed, at a loss, and isolated. In this area as well, temping can be helpful.

After the initial shock has worn off, it's important to take some positive action and get some positive results. If you've been unemployed for a while, you've probably sent out hundreds of résumés and have gotten back scores of polite form letters thanking you for your interest in their company. It can be a frustrating experience. Working as a temp can supply the positive results your ego needs. So, go sign up at a temporary staffing service. You'll feel better about yourself, and you will certainly get some work.

Of course, your goal is not to stay in-between jobs, but to be fully employed. You are actively looking for work. You can add another method to your job search and become a job seeker through temping. Or, you may like temping so much, you may stay a temp and make it a career—38 percent of all temps turn down full-time positions.

The Job Seeker

Whether you are in between jobs, re-entering the job market, or looking for your first job, temping can be the means to finding that full-time job, perhaps even a career. It has been shown that people who temp often get better, higher paying jobs because the pressure of earning a living while looking for work is reduced.

Carl was 40 years old and at his wit's end. Although he is a college graduate and was earning a Master's Degree, he had sent out over 100 résumés since losing his last job—with no results. He had a wife, who worked part time, and two young children. Finally, out of desperation, he took a transcription job at night that paid only $8 an hour. "It was strictly dead end," he says, "I was beginning to see myself in this for the rest of my life until I heard about temping. When I signed up, the coordinator took an interest in me and told me at the interview that I would be hired in no time at all, that I had the education, dressed impeccably, and that I would have the opportunity to be placed into a permanent position."

As fate would have it, it would take Carl more than two years to get a full-time job, during which time he had assignments at three companies, one for two years. "I stayed at that company because I felt there was an opportunity to get a full-time position. But, if there wasn't I could have always gotten another assignment. At least, now, I was paying the bills and the pressure was off."

Temping also offers an entree into a company that is just not possible to get any other way. Many companies list job openings in-house before placing them in the classifieds. There is also nothing to stop you from giving your résumé to the head of the department you are working in or to the company's human resources department. Of course, if you are offered a full-time position, you do have legal obligations to the temporary staffing service you are working for, which we'll discuss in chapter 8.

The best approach you can take is to work with the temporary staffing service or services you are signed up with. Tell them of your interests and industries in which you want to work. Chances are, they have temp work in that industry. Once you are on-site, you'll be in a good position to find out what is going on and to hear about possible openings.

Employers also will use a temporary worker to assess the need for a new full-time position. If you are that temporary worker, this gives the employer the opportunity to try you out in what is commonly called "temporary to full-time" arrangements. You can also use this trial period to test the potential employer to determine if the position will meet your long-term career goals and to see if the company's corporate culture is right for you.

If you are serious about finding a full-time job, temping may be a worthwhile approach. Just keep alert. Temping can bring unexpected opportunities and, for the entrepreneurial individual, open doors.

Changing Careers

Like the person who is between jobs and the job seeker, your object is to find a full-time position, although it would be in a field different from your present one. It's possible you've made a decision to change careers but you don't know exactly what other career you want to pursue. Temping gives you an opportunity to sample a variety of different industries and to get an insider's view of many different companies.

When Christina moved back to her hometown in Sacramento, California, she wanted to find something other than being the newspaper reporter she had been since graduating from college. "I just wanted to explore different areas where I wanted to go with my life and my second career," she says. Unfortunately, she found out that the corporate world did not necessarily welcome former journalists with open arms. She did land a job as a lobbyist but it wasn't for her. When things got financially desperate, she turned to the temp services. "Friends advised me to sign up with the services, but I didn't listen until things were getting pretty desperate. So I just applied to the services to see what they could offer and I was quite happy with how things worked out."

Christina was offered a couple of jobs that she didn't want and, because she was temping, didn't need to take. After testing the waters in a number of different industries and professions, she finally found what she was looking for. Christina is now employed full-time as a paralegal.

Christina signed up with six services to get as broad a perspective as possible. It is often the case that a service will have a majority of their accounts concentrated in one or very few industries. So, by signing up with a number of temporary help services, you increase your chances of learning about many career opportunities. Once again, it is important to communicate your desires to your personnel coordinator. In this case, however, you more than likely will be informing them of the industries you do not want to work in rather than the ones you do. Remember, it's not a problem to tell your service what you don't want to do. They will not hold it against you. It's their objective to place you in situations where you feel most comfortable and, therefore, most productive.

Extra Cash Wanted

Even if you already have a job, which is sufficient to take care of your necessities, it may not be enough to buy the "extra" things you want. These can range from a luxury item like that boat you've been dreaming of, or just replacing that noisy refrigerator. You could pull out the credit card, take a bank loan, or put a second mortgage on the house, but the cost of credit is going up and you don't really want to get into any more debt, do you?

Temping can be the solution for you. Unlike getting a part-time job, working as a temporary employee will give you extra money without having to make a commitment. So, when you've saved enough to buy what you wanted, you can just call the service and say you are no longer available. And that will be it. If six months later you want to make some extra money again, all you need do is call the service and put yourself back on the schedule. If you had previously proven your worth to them, they will be happy to have you back and, in short order, you'll be making money. This is certainly better than the alternative of having to look for another part-time job. Of course, chances are you might get used to that extra cash and never completely take yourself off the schedule.

A Second Income Required

Sadly, additional money is required to pay for necessities more often than to buy luxuries. More and more families find it impossible to manage basic needs on one income.

The U.S. Bureau of Labor Statistics reports that more than 50 percent of married couples are two-income families. The chances are that most of them do it because they need to do it. The cost of basic items such as food, clothing, medical care, and your children's education continues to escalate.

Working as a temporary employee can provide a permanent solution to some of your problems. It might sound strange to hear that working as a temp can provide something permanent, but that can be the case. The reason goes to the basic core of the temporary staffing services industry. Temporary help services appreciate and need employees who can make a consistent and regular commitment. If you have regular requirements, you will want to be on a regular schedule with your service. Your chances of working, therefore, will be greater. And both you and your service will be winners. You will make the extra money you need to help make ends meet and your service will have an employee they can count on.

The College Graduate

Many recent graduates are faced with the old Catch-22 situation. You know it: You can't get a job without experience, but you can't get experience without a job. Working as a temp can help you get around that by giving you work experience you can put on your résumé. If you know what you want to do, speak with your service. Your personnel coordinator will try to place you in the specific industries of your choice.

Once you find a company you like, temping can provide a back door to employment that you would otherwise be unable to open. You will have an opportunity to prove yourself and make yourself invaluable, thus overcoming the Catch-22. You will be able to make contacts from the inside and meet people you would never be able to meet if you tried to go through the front door of the human resources department.

Likewise, you will also find out from an inside perspective whether you really want to work for that company. For many people, a job is more than salary and benefits; it's environment, too. You will learn much more about a company while working for them as a temp than any employment advertisement or Dun & Bradstreet search will ever be able to tell you. You will learn how employees treat each other, how professional staff treats support staff, how professional staff treats other professional staff, and how managers treat subordinates. Are people treated with respect? Is there a feeling of pride among the employees? In short, you will gain an intimate knowledge of that company's corporate culture.

Or perhaps you don't have a clear idea of what you want to do with your college degree. Here again, temping will enable you to try a number of different areas, get a feel for what's going on, and help you make a choice. Each industry is different and each company within that industry has its own unique character and personality. By temping at several different companies, you will better be able to determine if the corporate culture at a specific company is the right one for you.

The Student

Why wait until after you graduate college? Why not work as a temporary employee while you're still in college? You will get a leg up on your fellow students, get some work experience, and help pay for your tuition costs.

You are already aware how much your education is costing you. You could take out plenty of student loans and end up deeply in debt for the first ten years of your adult life. That's one answer, but it might not be the best answer. If you are now a college student, you are most likely computer literate. Your skills will be a valuable asset in finding temporary work—work that will pay you a lot more than what you can usually find listed at your school's employment service.

You will also be able to get practical work experience in an office environment. This will help you land that first job and help you avoid the Catch-22 situation often faced by recent college graduates—even before you get into it.

That's what one Harvard Law School student did. Brian, who temped at office clerical positions while in college, wanted to see what the legal profession was like before he went to Harvard in September. So, the summer before he started Harvard, he left his home in New Jersey for Washington, DC, with nothing more than a list of temporary services specializing in the legal profession. "I went to DC, where it's difficult to get your foot in the door of a law firm just by walking in, without any kind of job at all."

Brian went to the first temporary legal service on his list. "They interviewed me and the benefit is they interview you on behalf of all their clients. So rather than go door-to-door to 50 different firms, which is time-consuming and impractical, I went there and they do the work for me."

Brian got a job the very next day with a large law firm that is headquartered in New York City. Not only did he have the chance to see the legal profession from a different perspective, he feels that his temp experience will greatly help him get an internship at this law firm as he progresses towards his juris doctorate. Brian would recommend temping to every college student. "Yes, definitely, I think it's a huge asset to college students because it's very difficult to find summer jobs, but not in the temp industry. It's a great benefit to college students."

In addition to gaining work experience, temping could be instrumental in helping you make a career choice. You will be able to explore different industries and companies before you determine where you would like to work. And, you will be able to maintain a schedule suited to your changing needs and requirements from semester to semester.

Need New Skills

"We can take a person who has never worked before and who doesn't have computer skills or really any skills at all. We can develop that person's skills so that he or she can enter the workforce," says Gretchen Kreske, information specialist of Manpower, Inc. headquartered in Milwaukee, Wisconsin. "We offer free computer training, so someone with no computer skills can come in and get the free training they need. And then we'll send them out on job assignments."

Yes, this does happen at temporary help services all across America. Temporary work can be ideal for people who need to upgrade their word processing skills or acquire new skills. According to a National Association of Temporary and Staffing Services survey, 66% of temporary workers reported they gained new skills while working as a temporary and 29% said they received more than twenty hours of training from their temporary help company.

In addition to direct, free training, you can practice on the service's equipment and go through software tutorials to upgrade your skills. When you feel comfortable with a new program, the service will let you test on it and, assuming you pass the test, will get you assignments for your newly acquired skills.

Temporary staffing companies are not being altruistic about giving you all this free training. It is in their best interests to make you as marketable as possible and to provide you with the skills their client companies demand. Why not take advantage of this situation and get a free upgrade, while earning extra cash in the process.

A Need for Flexibility

Perhaps you just need some flexibility in your life. The reasons can be varied and many. Maybe you need income, but you also need time to take care of an elderly parent. Or you are a single parent. For 2 million working mothers, for example, temporary work has proven the best way of staying employed while they raise a family. Do you like to travel? Whatever your personal reasons, working with a temporary help service company can be the means to achieving your end. As a temporary worker, the possibility of maintaining a work schedule suited to your requirements is greatly increased.

Freedom and flexibility are the most frequently cited reasons for working as a temporary. The very nature of temporary work implies choice. You are free to choose your hours, your days, your vacations, and your assignments. You can work as little or as much as you like. Of course, your ability to get work when you want it is a product of supply and demand and geographic location. In large urban areas, where there is a large demand and where industries work around the clock, your chances of tailoring a schedule to fit you are better. In smaller towns, this may be a bit more difficult.

Nonetheless, if freedom and flexibility are your goals, then temporary work is something you should definitely explore. In fact, it may be the only industry that can satisfy your needs.

The Creative Person

One group that has traditionally needed flexibility in their lives are people involved in a creative or artistic pursuit. If you are an actor, writer, singer, dancer, musician, or artist, you will appreciate the flexibility temping affords you. Also, unlike other jobs that creative people tend to do, such as waiting tables, there will always be a job waiting for you should you need to take an extended period of time off—to do that six-month road show, or to write a book, like this one, for example.

Temporary staffing service companies have a long history of dealing with creative people, especially in large cities. They appreciate your dedication to your particular field of creative endeavor and know you are quite capable of translating that dedication into responsible work performance. They also know that you are the ones most likely to be awake and ready to go when that urgent 11 p.m. call comes in from a company looking for someone right away who can work for ten hours. As a group, creative people make extremely successful temporary workers.

The Newcomer

American society is one of the most mobile groups in the world. According to *American Demographics*, about 17 million of us move annually. Perhaps you will be one of them. Or maybe your spouse's firm will move and you will be forced to make the move also. Temping can help smooth the transition and help replace the income you may lose.

Becky became the consummate newcomer and part of a temping couple when she joined her fiancé, Jamie, who was working as a locum tenens physician (a doctor who works as a temp). We'll hear more about Jamie in the chapter on High-End Temping, but, right now, let's talk about Becky. Becky joined her fiancé on the road when she was just finishing her Ph.D. in industrial psychology. Having a partner whose assignments lasted no more than six weeks before they would have to move to a different city made it impossible for her to look for a full-time position. Fortunately, Becky was also computer literate.

As soon as she got to where Jamie was on assignment, she signed up with a national temporary help service and got work almost immediately. "I worked temp while Jamie worked locums," she says. "It was ideal for me and I got work almost immediately everywhere we went." In fact, Becky's arrangement was so successful for her that one medical center she was assigned to hired her as a consultant to do a follow-up study based on the company's meeting her and getting to know her as a temp.

If you already are working for a national temporary staffing service, all you need to do is have your records transferred to their office in your destination city. If you are not, sign up at a service that has an office where you want to relocate before you move. Even if you have no actual work history with that particular company, just having your test scores transferred will save you time and effort when you move. As soon as you get to where you're going, call up the staffing company and make an appointment to meet with them.

The Returnee

The children are out of the house and for the first time in eighteen years you have some time on your hands. Perhaps you would like to put that time to use by earning some extra money. The problem is you haven't been in an office environment for many years and your office skills are rusty. Not to mention you probably have no computer skills at all.

That was Helen's problem exactly. Although she was a teacher by profession, she got married shortly after she received her Master's Degree and after teaching for just two years, decided to leave the workforce when her first child was born. "I didn't want to go back into teaching;

I'd been away too long," she says. "I wanted to do something, but the idea of working in an office was intimidating."

This is where a temp service can be very helpful and should probably be your number one choice if you are returning to the job market after a long absence. Temporary help services offer a range of jobs for a wide variety of skill levels. They will most likely be able to fit you into a position that matches your current experience. A temporary staffing service is primarily looking for reliable and responsible people. They will definitely look upon your experience as a homemaker and child rearer favorably, understanding that the skills you put to use in the home are easily transferable to the workplace.

In Helen's case, her education was obviously a plus. Still, she started life as a temp doing general filing and some reception work. "I liked being out of the house and feeling productive," she says. After a while, Helen took the opportunity to become computer literate and now takes on some word processing assignments.

Once you've gotten your foot in the door and have had a taste of the working life, you may want to take advantage of the many opportunities temporary help services offer to upgrade your skills as Helen did. You will become a bigger asset to your service and make more money.

The Retiree

Studies indicate that retirees are one of the most experienced groups of workers in America. In one study commissioned by the Commonwealth Fund in 1991, it was found that retirees pay more attention to customers, take fewer days off and stay longer on the job. Many retirees already work full or part time. Many more would like to. A poll conducted by the American Association of Retired Persons reported that Americans aged 55-64 prefer work to retirement by a three to one margin.

A need to still feel productive is not the only reason you may want to work. Unfortunately, you may also need to work because your pension and Social Security Income benefits do not stretch that far. Living on a fixed income can cause stresses and hardships all its own, something commonly called "pension-tension."

Evelyn, aged 65, who was a customer service manager in the retail furniture industry before she retired, has found temping to be the ideal situation to meet her needs. Like so many people, her Social Security and pension just don't reach far enough, but she also wants to enjoy life on her terms in her golden years. "I've been temping since October 1994 because my retirement is not sufficient to support me, even with Social Security," says Evelyn. "But I want to enjoy my life, too. So, I work temporary for a while, save some money, and then I quit working and do something I want to do, like play or go to school. That's the way I intend to live for the duration of my life, and I find it really works for me."

Evelyn does strictly secretarial work. As a former manager, she does not want to be saddled with too much responsibility and the temp service is more than happy to accommodate her. "It's a great way to go for people in my position."

If you are looking for a way to feel productive or need to find a way to make ends meet, or both, temping may provide you with the best choice between full-time work and full-time retirement. The money you earn as a temp can be used to supplement your Social Security benefits. Receiving benefits does not mean you cannot work. They will not be affected until your earnings go above a certain amount. At that point, you can stop accepting assignments. Your temp service will be happy to work with you and perhaps even be willing to inform you when you have reached your threshold. For more information on your earnings limit or any questions you may have about Social Security, contact your local Social Security office.

Even if money is not an issue, spending a set amount of time in a working environment may help structure your life and still give you the flexibility to customize a work schedule suitable to your needs.

You should never feel that you are too old to be hired or that your skills are too out of date. The temporary help service won't feel that way. Your personnel coordinator will be able to find something that's suitable to you. Many temporary help companies have programs designed to recruit mature workers and help them get back into the workforce. Companies also appreciate the experience and work ethic you bring to the job.

Many seniors who like to travel may also find a temporary service an extremely useful resource. By signing up with a nationwide staffing service, you will be able to travel and work at the same time. You might even be able to pay for your trip and expenses this way.

"I'm Fed Up"

Arthur was an attorney for ten years in a couple of firms when he was offered a partnership track. "They wanted me to work, 60, 70, 80 hours a week, something insane," he says. But at that moment of truth, Arthur had a vision. "What flashed before my eyes was that I could do this and nothing else, or I could leave." Arthur left.

In plain truth, though, Arthur had become disgusted with the tremendous and all-consuming requirements of his career. "Being a lawyer in the way I had come to know it, had become either boring or aversive," he says. After a stint on the unemployment line, Arthur turned to legal temping as an option. "Temping somehow had this ring of doing a little bit and then seeing what else you can do."

Through temping, Arthur found a way to practice his profession without the hassles. We'll hear more about Arthur later on in this book and

39

find out about the expanding opportunities for professionals in the temping industry.

How many people are out there who are just fed up and are looking to scale down their stress level, even at the cost of their income level? Nobody knows the answer. But we can assume there are many. Perhaps you are one of them. And maybe you feel trapped in what you are doing. Give temping a try. It may prove to be a viable alternative.

If you are the type of person who is fed up with office politics, then temping may also be right for you. This is not to say you will never get involved in office politics again. After all, politics is about people and you will always have to deal with people. But, as a temp, you will have the option of letting the hassles of office politics "roll off your back." Temping is truly the kind of job you can leave at the office when your work day ends.

A Job Not!

More and more, people are finding the "temp lifestyle" a preferable choice to getting a full-time job. The reasons may vary and we've already looked at a number of possible explanations—insecurities in the job market, a need for flexibility, a desire to have less stress. I know of one temp, for example, who has worked at the same client company for three years. Why would she do that and forego the benefits of being a full-time employee? Simple. She likes the idea of being able to take a few months off each year to travel, knowing that when she returns the company will gladly take her back. In the meantime, her staffing service places someone else in that position during her absence. It's like having a job, while still not having a job. It's a job not!

Whatever the individual reasons, more than one third of temporary workers turn down full-time positions in favor of remaining a temp. These people are called career temps. A career temp is someone who has been in the industry for a while and is highly skilled. They have made a reputation for themselves and can count on steady work, whether they take long-term or short-term assignments.

Perhaps you see yourself as wanting to belong to this elite group of temps. We'll take a closer look at career temping in chapter 10 and find out what it takes to become one. Then, you will better be able to decide if career temping is right for you.

If you've seen yourself in one of the categories or heard yourself in some of the people who temp, then temping may be just the thing you are looking for. But, even if you didn't, that doesn't mean that temping isn't right for you. You may have very unique needs and requirements and in the large playing field that makes up the temporary industry, there's something for just about everybody.

The following chapter will take a closer look at how a temporary service operates and the extensive variety of jobs being offered. I'm sure you'll find something that fits you to a "T"—as in Temp.

4

The Role of the Temporary Help Service

Temporary services have filled a unique role in the labor market since the 1890s, when industrial temporaries first began to appear on the shipping docks of Milwaukee, Wisconsin. By the 1920s, temps were filling in for full-time office and clerical workers in Chicago, Illinois. During World War II, with 17 million men registering for the war effort and women leaving their clerical positions to take higher paying factory jobs, temporary help firms filled the void in offices by recruiting previously unemployed housewives for these office/clerical positions. After the war, temporaries, as they then officially became known, were found to be valuable for replacing absent regular employees and for maintaining staff during peak production cycles.

One hundred years has seen a lot of growth in the temporary worker industry, most of it in the past two decades. Today, the industry employs more than 2.2 million men and women, has gross revenues of more than $39.2 billion per year and has become the third fastest-growing service business in the U.S. Some of the largest private employers in the U.S. are, in fact, temporary help services.

What Exactly Is a Temporary Help Service Company?

Despite the recent surge in the number of temporary workers, the exact nature of a temporary service company is often misunderstood.

A Temporary Help Service Is an Employer: There is some confusion between a temporary employment service and an employment agency. When an employment agency sends you to a company, it is for the purpose of you becoming employed by that company. You are paid by the company and the employment agency charges the company a fee for finding you. It may or may not charge you a fee. When a temporary employment service sends you to a company, it, in effect, "assigns" you to that company for a specified period of time. When the assignment ends, you can then be reassigned to another company. It charges the company an hourly rate for your services. You are never charged. In addition to being responsible for paying your salary, your service is also legally responsible for withholding required income taxes and Social Security and for paying Workers' Compensation, disability, and Unemployment Insurance. On the other hand, the mere act of signing up with a service does not automatically make you an employee of that service. The service has no legal obligation to you until you are assigned work. That certainly can be confusing.

A Temporary Help Service Is a Middleman: On the one side there are client companies with requirements; on the other side, employees with skills. The temporary help service puts both together to form a match. The service exercises no control over the needs and requirements of its client companies. The best it can do is keep abreast of what the market needs and find employees that are capable of meeting those demands. They find new employees through advertising in newspapers and by offering bonuses to current employees who bring new people into the company. New employees are interviewed and tested. When a company calls, the service presumably has a person ready to fill that spot. If it doesn't, a company will soon find another service to call.

A Temporary Help Service Is a Business: It is fundamentally understood that a corporation is in business to make money, but when it comes to temporary help services, that same understanding seems to be lacking generally. Perhaps it is because the product a temporary help service sells is you—the temp—and people don't like to be considered products. One hears disgruntled talk among temporary workers about the markup that services get for the temps' labor. But, when all overhead factors are taken into account, the profit margin of a temporary service is no greater than what you or I would want if we were in business. If there is any problem on the business side of the industry, it is that, except for some minor administrative costs, there is not much downside for a service to be overstaffed (except for being known as a company that can't get its employees enough work). All things considered, there is an obvious incentive for a service company to have as many available employees as possible. Your goal is to be the one getting the assignments. That's what this book is about.

The Different Types of Services

Now that you have some idea of what a temporary help service company is, let's take a look at the different types of services that you can sign up with. In general, there are three categories of services:

Temporary Staffing Service: This is the one we will discuss most frequently in this book. As noted earlier, a temporary staffing service hires its own employees and then assigns them to client companies for specific periods of time. The service makes sure that its employees are skilled in the areas the client requires and has the ability to perform the job function. The client company is responsible for the day-to-day supervision of the employee and to make sure the assigned work gets done.

Temporary-to-Full-Time Service: Also called "temp to perm," this type of service combines the speed and flexibility of a temporary staffing service with the job-finding capacity of an employment agency. In recent years, so many temporary staffing services have instituted temp-to-perm procedures that the line between a temporary service and a temp-to-perm service has all but disappeared. Nonetheless, if you want to get full-time work, you should make sure the service you sign up with has such opportunities. Unlike a traditional employment agency, you first work for the client company as a temporary worker until you are officially hired by the company. This is a good way for you and the company to evaluate each other and to see if there is a good match. You are never charged a fee in a temp-to-perm arrangement. You may be charged a fee with a traditional employment agency. We'll take a closer look at this method in chapter 9.

Long-Term Staffing: Also called "facilities staffing," this type of service specializes in placing individuals on long-term, indefinite assignments. More and more companies budget positions as "temp" positions. These positions will never be filled by full-time employees. For example, I once worked for a major corporation whose word processing center for one of their divisions was made up entirely of temps working on a long-term, indefinite basis. If you are interested only in long-term work, this is the type of service you should sign up with.

As you can see, there are quite a few types of services to choose from. But the general categories don't begin to tell the full story of a temporary help company. Within each category there are subcategories. Most services end up specializing in different job descriptions and in different industries. There are temporary help services that specialize in placing word processors, writers, health-care workers, or computer analysts. There are services that have the majority of their accounts in the financial industry, the advertising industry, or the aerospace industry. Even some of the largest and best services are known to handle some areas better than other areas, just like a restaurant with an extensive menu is known to make one or two dishes better than the rest of its fare. All of these factors need to be considered when you are shopping around for a temporary service that's right for you.

Where Is the Work?

Dependingon your skills and preferences, there is an almost unlimited number of different types of assignments available through temping in an equally unlimited number of industries. More than 100 different positions are filled each day from unskilled labor to highly skilled technical positions. Likewise, just about every industry uses temporary workers. To name just a few, they include the banking and financial industries, advertising and publishing, the construction industry, the medical field, the legal profession, the non-profit sector, the insurance industry, retail, fashion, high-tech, and telecommunications.

Office and clerical jobs are the most abundant positions available to temporary workers and this is not likely to change. Other fields, however, are expanding rapidly. These include the technical field, which now makes up thirteen percent of the industry, and the medical field, now about eleven percent. The professional area, made up of job categories such as CEO, accountant, and attorney, is on the rise with five percent of the industry.

Let's take a closer look at the five main areas available to temporary workers, the specific jobs available in each, and the outlook for future growth:

Office/Clerical Positions

There is no question that office/clerical positions are the largest area of the temporary industry, accounting for almost 40% of all positions filled by temporary service companies. Since every industry has need for office/clerical personnel, this area is also the most versatile. Positions include:

- Word Processor
- Data Entry Operator
- Desktop Publishing Operator
- Data Coding Clerk
- Secretary
- Administrative Assistant
- General Office Clerk
- Clerk Typist
- Receptionist
- Paralegal
- Proofreader
- Transcriber
- Product Demonstrator
- Telephone Salesperson

- Sales Clerk
- Messenger
- Mail Clerk

Future Growth: In general, office/clerical positions will increasingly demand computer skills as office automation continues. Even positions that were considered semi-skilled a few years ago, such as mail clerk, will require the technical knowledge needed to run computerized mail-sorting equipment. To stay competitive in this field, it's almost a given that the more software programs you know, the better position you will be in to compete. Bobby Riggins of Talent Tree Staffing Services notes, "A key change over the last several years has been the request from our clients for employees to be proficient with multiple software packages versus one individual package."

You should be well versed in a number of Microsoft Windows™ word processing programs such as Microsoft Word™ and WordPerfect for Windows™. Knowledge of that old stand-by WordPerfect 5.1 for DOS™ should also be one of the things on your knowledge list. Increasingly, temporary workers are also being called upon to work with spreadsheet and graphics programs. In addition, you should have a working knowledge of the operating system. If you work in this area but are not quite up to snuff, take advantage of the free skills training that is offered by most temporary service companies. Speak to your personnel coordinator about learning the latest programs. Those that keep up on the latest technology will get the highest paying jobs; those that don't may find it difficult to get any work at all.

Among other positions in this category, the Bureau of Labor Statistics, Office of Employment Projections, notes that general office clerks will be among the occupations with the largest job growth into the year 2005, increasing by 24 percent. Retail salespeople will also grow by an estimated 24 percent. The BLS also notes that the paralegal profession will increase by 88 percent by the year 2005, making it one of the fastest growing occupations in the U.S. It should also be noted, however, that paralegals without computer skills will find it difficult to compete with paralegals with computer skills.

Industrial Positions

These positions still make up a hefty chunk of the temporary worker market—25 percent. Industrial positions include:

- Bindery Worker
- Circuit Board Assembly Machine Operator
- Assembler
- Construction Worker
- Manufacturing Employee
- Shipping and Receiving Clerk
- Maintenance/Janitorial Work
- Pipefitter
- Electrician
- Millwright

Future Growth: According to the BLS employment outlook for the years 1992-2005, within the goods-producing sector, only construction will add jobs due to employment growth. The total share of manufacturing jobs is also expected to decline according to the same forecast, although manufacturing jobs will still account for one of every seven jobs in the U.S. by the year 2005. Janitors and cleaners are among the occupations with the largest job growth—nineteen percent increase—for the years 1992 to 2005.

Medical Positions

Temporary workers in the medical field make up about seven percent of the total, but this field is rapidly expanding. These positions include:

- Home Health Aide
- Registered Nurse
- Licensed Practical Nurse
- Lab Technician
- Medical Technologist

Future Growth: As a group, this field is one of the most rapid areas of growth among all categories of temporary workers and this is expected to continue for many years to come. According to the Bureau of Labor Statistics, home health aide is the number one fast-growing profession in the U.S. today and will continue to grow at a phenomenal rate into the year 2005. Registered nurse and nurse's aide are also among the nation's booming professions. These statistics will translate over into the temporary employment sector as well. Temps in this category can expect to be able to demand top salaries, steady work, and the ability to choose the kind of scheduling that is most appropriate to their individual needs. If and when a national health-care bill is passed by Congress, an additional positive effect on this occupational category can be expected.

Technical Positions

Thirteen percent of all of temp openings are for technical workers. These positions include:

- Engineer
- Computer Programmer

- Laboratory Technician
- Technical Writer/Editor
- Systems Analyst
- Chemist

Future Growth: It probably wouldn't surprise anyone to find systems analyst in both the Bureau of Labor Statistics top ten list of fastest growing occupations and occupations with the largest growth. Also on that list are computer engineer and scientist. The technical area is especially fitted to a temp lifestyle since many jobs in this field are project specific. It can be reasonably assumed that corporations will increasingly view the use of technical temps as a very cost-effective way of doing business.

Professional Positions

Professional positions still comprise a relatively small but rapidly expanding segment of temporary workers; however, the press coverage that this group receives has certainly made temping a more acceptable option on all levels. It is now quite clear that temping can fit the needs and requirements of just about every educational level, ability, and expertise. Job titles in this category include:

- Accountant
- Attorney
- Doctor
- Pharmacist
- Middle & Senior Management, including CEO, CFO, and COO
- Sales & Marketing Professional

Future Growth: Bryce A. Arrowood, president of LawCorps® Legal Staffing Services (a company that deals with legal temps, including attorneys, in Washington, DC), expects the professional niche market to boom. Says Arrowood, "I expect all professional niches will continue to grow at a rapid rate as corporate America becomes more convinced of and comfortable with the high-caliber, high-quality professional temporary personnel available in today's market." The numbers bear him out. In 1993, professional temping comprised 7.8 percent of the total temporary market. It now comprises 9 percent of the market and is expected to grow at the rate of 35 percent a year.

We'll take a look at professional temping in chapter 11, "High-End Temping."

Salaries and Benefits

Unlike a permanent job where you know upfront what your salary will be from week to week, your temp salary can vary from assignment to assignment and from client company to client company—even for the same job skills. It is not possible, therefore, for you to think about salary in the traditional way. It is better to think of your salary in terms of a range, going from the lowest rate you will work for to the highest rate you can make. For example, a word processor may earn anywhere from $525 per week to a top of $600 per week, doing the same job in the same city in the same shift. While this may make it difficult to figure out your monthly income, it is best to use the lower figure of your range to determine if you will be able to pay your bills.

Because the skills needed for temporary employees are the same skills required for full-time employees, salaries can be equal to, and in some cases, greater than those paid to full-timers. In general, the salary range depends on a number of factors:

Your Skills: Salaries are consistent with the type of work you do. A mail clerk will make less than a word processor.

Your Geographical Location: States like New York and California have higher pay scales for temporary workers than other parts of the country. Large urban areas pay higher wages than small towns. In general, the higher the cost of living in the area, the higher the salary you can expect to receive.

Your Seniority with the Service: Most services will give you a raise after you've been with them for six months. But it will be up to you to ask. Don't expect the service to voluntarily give you a raise. In addition, people who have been with the service usually get first crack at the higher paying assignments.

Your Ability to Negotiate: Don't be shy. If you get a call for an assignment and you feel the pay is too low, ask for more money. You can sometimes get a higher rate by negotiating aggressively.

Supply and Demand: Whatever your skills, if they are in short supply in your area, you can expect to get paid top dollar for what you do. It does seem that even entry-level people with minimal skills will be in short supply in the coming years. This should put temporary workers in an even better bargaining position. The demand for people with skills never goes down. Also, when unemployment is low, temp salaries tend to rise.

The following table will give you an idea of the salary ranges you can expect to find in some popular temp categories:

Some Sample Salaries		
Job Title	*Region*	*Salary Range*
Administrative Assistant	Atlanta	$9 and up/hour

Job Title	Region	Salary Range
Receptionist	Atlanta	$6.50 and up/ hour
Word Processor	New York City	$16 - $27/hour
Office Clerk	New York City	$6 - $8/hour
Receptionist	New York City	$8 - $10/hour
Graphics Designer	National average	$11.45 - $20/hour
Bookkeeper	National average	$10.73 - $12/hour
Experienced paralegal/ law clerk	Washington, DC	$10-$16/hour
Attorney	New York City	Up to $120/hour

Sources: Personal experience, Winston Staffing Services, Inc., Norrell Services, LawCorps® Legal Staffing Services, Talent Tree Staffing Services, Special Counsel International

For some, salaries may not be an issue, but benefits, such as health insurance, may be. While most temps cite freedom and flexibility as some of the key reasons they temp, benefits have become more important as focus has shifted from temping out of desire to temping out of necessity. Former full-time employees who came to expect health coverage and pension plans provided by their employers are looking to their services for these types of benefits.

The concerns of these temporary employees are being heard by the temporary help industry, and many companies now provide some basic form of group health plan. Nevertheless, 92 percent of temps do not have health insurance and 98 percent do not have pension plans or cannot obtain a 401(k) tax-deferred retirement plan. It can be assumed that temporary services, in order to remain competitive, will offer these benefits on a more regular and obtainable basis in the future.

Let's take a look at some of the benefits that are being offered now and, where possible, some alternatives you may want to consider. Bear in mind that you become eligible for most of these benefits after you have worked for the service a certain number of hours. That number can vary, but it is typically between 1,200 and 1,500 hours in a 12-month period. (Working a 40-hour week would add up to 2,080 hours per year.) Of course, you have to put in those hours with one service. Your benefits will stay in effect as long as you are working for that particular service but, again, you should check with the service to see what their requirements are.

There are some 6,000 temporary help service companies in the U.S., and not all of the benefits discussed in the following list are offered by all of the services. Many are just offered by the larger services, but, bear in mind, there are some excellent small services out there that have good assignments, even though they may not offer the benefits of the big-boys. Unless benefits are an absolute priority, you shouldn't cross out the small services on that basis alone.

> **Major Medical and Hospitalization:** Most services now offer employees group plans covering medical expenses and hospital stays. While group rates are less expensive than individual rates, you still have to pay the full cost of coverage. You normally have to be employed by the service for 30 days before you are eligible to purchase a plan through them. Plans can be purchased on a long-term or short-term basis. Very few of the larger services will pay part of the premium. However, you have to work a certain number of hours to be eligible. Some services offer discount dental and prescription plans as well.

> **An Alternative Medical and Hospital Plan:** It's sometimes not easy to meet the minimum requirements for obtaining this important benefit, especially if you use a number of different services. And with all the freedom and choice of services, you may not want to stick with one service for a long period of time. One alternative to obtaining medical and hospital benefits through your temporary employment

service—which may be contingent upon how many hours you work in a given period—is to find group coverage on your own. There are professional and social associations that you can join, which, for a modest annual membership fee, will offer group coverage. I once joined a social organization, which for $40 per year dues, gave me access to group medical and dental insurance. HMO plans are also worth looking into and are usually less expensive than buying individual health insurance.

Life Insurance: Some services do offer life insurance as well as accidental death and dismemberment insurance.

Pension Plans: One of the major benefits of being a full-time employee that is sadly lacking in the temporary worker industry is access to pension plans. However, one service is rolling out a pension plan shortly and once that happens, other services will probably follow. For now, though, if you plan on temping on a long-term basis, your best bet is to set up a tax-free savings plan by opening up an Individual Retirement Account (IRA) or a Keogh plan.

Holiday and Vacation Pay: Vacation pay is based on a minimum number of hours worked in the previous year. The number is usually around 1,500 for 40 hours of paid vacation. Holiday pay is figured on a minimum number of hours worked during a specified period of time before the holiday. This is something on the order of 500 hours in the preceding sixteen weeks prior to the holiday and work during the week of the holiday. All those numbers and hours are pretty confusing to me, and I get the feeling you have to be a rocket scientist to keep track of it all. While I've met temps who have gotten vacation pay, I've never met one who got paid for a holiday. If anyone was eligible, he or she was most likely unaware of it, and many services don't seem to track these things for the employee. In any case, I've never met anyone who went into temping for the holiday pay. In fact, it's better to work on a holiday and get that holiday pay rate.

Incentive Bonuses: There are all types of incentive bonuses out there. Some services pay a bonus to employees who complete long-term projects, rewarding that person for helping to reduce the turnover rate. There are bonuses for accepting a hard-to-fill position. Performance bonuses, which are based on a number of criteria, such as good client evaluations, recommendation by your personnel coordinator, and a certain number of hours worked, are also available at some services. And just about all services will pay you a bonus when you refer a qualified applicant to them. The amount of the bonus is based on the person's skill level and is payable after that person has completed a minimum number of hours.

Free Skills Courses: One of the biggest benefits is the ability to upgrade your skills and to stay on top of the latest technology. Services conduct formal and informal classes in computer and administrative skills. You can take advantage of this opportunity and increase your marketability.

Stock-Option Plans: Many publicly traded services offer their employees the option to buy company stock at a discount. It's a good way for you to save some money, perhaps make some money if the stock goes up, and feel like you belong to an organization. Stock-option plans are usually available after you've worked for the company for a period of time, usually one full year of continuous service.

To a lesser extent, temporary help services may also provide a credit union service, day-care availability, tuition reimbursement, and travel and hotel discounts.

In the United States, your temporary help service is also your legal employer and is subject to all the rules and regulations governing an employer. It is required to cover you under the Workers' Compensation and disability laws. You are also eligible to collect Unemployment Insurance benefits when you meet the minimum levels set by your state. You should check with your State Unemployment Division for more information about eligibility requirements.

> **A Word About Unemployment Insurance:** A few states are now tightening the rules of eligibility for temp workers who apply for Unemployment Insurance. The new laws require a temp to contact their temporary employment service within five working days after completion of an assignment for reassignment. Any temp who does not contact the service would be disqualified for unemployment benefits.

The reason? People. It seems that a few temps work just long enough to collect unemployment benefits. As soon as they reach the minimum level, they never contact the service again. By failing to report to the service, they have, in a very real sense, voluntarily quit, which is not a valid reason for receiving benefits in any state. The fact is, the temporary service industry claims to lose millions of dollars a year in questionable unemployment claims. Personally, I feel if there's work to be done, then I shouldn't be eligible to collect. Of course, if you are told by your service that there are no assignments available, you may still legitimately file for Unemployment Insurance benefits. But most temps just move on to another service. The question really comes down to one of practicality. The chances are good that any service will fight your unemployment claim. Is it really worth the fight when there are so many services out there with sufficient work for you? If you choose to fight for unemployment, the chances are higher that you will lose that service as a resource than that you will collect. Is it really worth the struggle?

We've seen in this chapter the types of services that are out there, the kinds of positions they deal in, and the services that are offered. Since there are so many services, each with their own clientele and benefits packages, picking the right one or ones for you is critical to your success as a temp. In the following chapter, we'll discuss how to go about the process of choosing the right service for you.

CHAPTER 5

What Temporary Help Service is Right for You?

As you can see from the previous chapter, there is enough diversity and opportunity in the temporary worker industry to suit just about anyone's needs. Because there are so many temporary help services— many of which specialize in different job categories, different industries, and even different companies within industries—selecting the right service for you is integral to getting the most out of your temping experience.

What Do I Want from Temping?

The best way to start the service selection process is to ask yourself what it is you need most from temping. The following questions are designed to help you determine that:

Why Do I Need to Temp? This might seem like an obvious question, but there are some situations that, with a little foresight, can mean the difference between getting a job quickly or not. Planned activities such as relocating to a new city, retiring, or traveling lend themselves to establishing yourself with a service before you start the activity. If you are planning on moving, for example, and you don't have a job, registering with a service that has an office in your new location will save you a lot of time. If your unemployment insurance is about to run out, signing up with a service before that happens can avoid a financial catastrophe.

What Are My Skills? Unless you are only looking for professional or technical assignments, do not limit yourself when you take stock of your skills. Temporary help service companies have long been in the business of employing people who have not been in the job market for a long time or who are just breaking into the job market. Even unused or rusty skills can be an asset when seeking temporary employment. Life skills are also valuable. Homemakers, for example, have organizational skills they can put to good use as a temp. Having a pleasant phone manner can mean getting quick work as a receptionist. Include volunteer work, hobbies, and any adult education classes. Whatever your assets, paint yourself with a broad brush.

Computer skills are in great demand. If you already have them, you are one step ahead of the game. If not, you may wish to take a computer course. Or, you can wait until you sign up with a service and take advantage of their free skills upgrading program. Either way, the faster you can come up to speed on computer knowledge, the more marketable you will be. Let's face it, even executives need to have a working knowledge of computers in today's job market.

What Kind of Work Can I Do? Once you have listed your skills, hone in on the skills that seem most marketable. A good way to match your skills with what is needed in the marketplace is to check the classified advertisements in your local newspaper to see what the temporary help service companies are looking for. Remember, unless you are temping to fulfill some personal dream, your goal is to make money out of temping. As in any business, the best way to make money is to find the need and fill it.

How Much Money Do I Need? Aside from the fact that your skills have a certain market value and, therefore, a definite pay range, it's important when thinking about temping to have an accurate idea of the amount of money you need to pay bills or to accomplish your goals. As we've already seen, temping assignments can have a salary range, even for the same position in the same city. You must also face the possibility that there might not always be work when you need it. It's important, therefore, to have a bottom line number in mind before you sign up with any service.

What Kind of Work Do I Want to Do? There is a difference between the kind of work you can do and the kind of work you want to do. Temping can give you an excellent opportunity to try out a new career, test new skills, or reuse old skills. You can use temping as a stepping stone to something different. When it comes time for the interview, be sure to mention the kind of work you most want to do. Your personnel coordinator can be a great help in getting you from where you are to where you want to be.

Am I Willing to Travel? Professional and technical positions may involve extensive travel and being away from home for long periods of time. Is this acceptable to you? If not, then you will have to inform the service about your needs at the time you sign up.

Other positions may involve traveling outside of your immediate area. Do you own a car? Are you willing to use it to get to work? Do you have a good public transportation system in your area? How far would you travel to a temp assignment? five miles? Ten miles? 25 miles?

When Can I Work? Depending on your area, assignments may be available 24 hours a day, seven days a week. Are you willing to work nights and/or weekends? These assignments pay the most, but your own personal lifestyle may not allow you to accept this kind of position. Are there any days or hours you cannot work for personal or religious reasons?

Selecting a Service

Depending on the area of the country you live in, there can be a hundred temporary services to choose from. Selecting the one or ones that are right for you can be a daunting task. Here are several ways to begin:

Ask a Friend: If you know someone who already works as a temporary worker in the field you want to work in, ask that person to offer some recommendations and to describe his or her experiences. Make sure that your friend's needs are similar to your own. Your friend may be happy to work three days a week while you need to work five, for example.

Ask a Former Employer: With the extensive use of temporary workers today, just about every employer has had some contact with a service or two. Speak to the person who is in charge of contracting with a temporary service to find out which ones in your area the company has dealt with and what their experience has been.

The Classified Section of Your Local Newspaper: You'll see quite a few of the larger services advertising for employees and the skills they are looking for. They have big, splashy ads that seem very inviting. You can also find them under the specific job category listings. Bear in mind, though, that just because a service is advertising does not necessarily mean they are busy. It is in their best interests to have as many people signed up as possible. The one difference between calling one of these services and applying for a regular job is that a service will never tell you not to come in.

The Yellow Pages: Temporary help companies are listed under Employment Contractors—Temporary Help. The larger services place display ads in the Yellow Pages, listing the kind of work they have.

What the ads and the Yellow Pages don't tell you is if they have enough work in your field to keep you busy. They don't tell you if you will be treated properly. They don't tell you what their benefits are. These are things you'll have to find out for yourself. You should not ignore all those services in the Yellow Pages that list only a name, address, and telephone number. There are many fine small services that may just be right for you. I worked for years with a service that handled only word processors and had just a couple of accounts. But they treated me well and got me the amount of work I needed, when I needed it.

Don't overwhelm yourself by getting too many names at once. Remember, if you live in a big city there can be hundreds of services to choose from. It's probably a good idea to keep it down to ten. Once you have ten, it's time to get on the phone and make some calls.

The Initial Contact

Your initial contact with the service on the phone is critical in helping you determine if that service is right for you. Remember, the same people who answer the phone for you also answer the phone when a client company calls. Put yourself in the client company's position and ask yourself if you would want to do business with that service. Is the phone answered promptly? Does the person answering the phone sound professional and courteous? Do they keep you on hold for a long time? Is the person on the other end of the phone willing to answer your questions? Your first impressions will help you determine whether the service is people-oriented or treats you like a number. Before setting up an appointment, you may wish to call the service and do an exploratory investigation to see if the service is right for you by asking the following questions:

- Does the service specialize in certain kinds of assignments?

- Do they have jobs in the industry or industries you are interested in working in?

- Do they have temp-to-perm opportunities? Many services do not have formal temp-to-perm procedures, but they can inform you if they have clients who regularly seek full-time employees.

- What kind of benefits do they offer? Not all services are equal in this regard. But, unless benefits are really important, I would not count out a service based on benefits at this stage.

- How long do they expect the sign-up process to take?

- What is the salary range for the assignments you want?

- There is no point in asking if they have work because the service will tell you they do. It is a rare service that will tell you they are slow right now and there's no point in coming in.

- You may also wish to ask if the service is a member of the National Association of Temporary and Staffing Services (NATSS). NATSS is a voluntary association of approximately 1,400 staffing services nationwide. Members pay a fee to join. Membership in NATSS is not necessarily a recommendation for that service, but I would certainly wonder about a service that answered this question with a "What's NATSS?"

For information about NATSS, please write to:

National Association of Temporary and Staffing Services
119 South Saint Asaph Street
Alexandria, VA 22314-3119

Or visit them on the World Wide Web at:

http://www.natss.com/staffing

- Another place you may want to check out is the local Better Business Bureau to see if any complaints have been filed against the service.

Narrowing Down the List

Now that you've made your calls, you can check the answers you received against the criteria you have established for yourself. Does the service sound, on this initial contact, like it can give you the kind of work you want at an acceptable salary range? Keep in mind, though, that what is equally important to the answers is **how** the questions were answered. Were they answered with courtesy? Or, did the person at the other end sound like you were wasting his or her time? Remember that if a service is busy, you may be put on hold often. That may be a good sign that the service has work. What you're looking for in this initial contact is the way in which your questions are answered.

Once you're satisfied that you've found some services that appeal to you, it's time to call them back and make appointments.

It is not a good idea to make more than two appointments on any given day. Between the testing and interviewing, I have spent as long as four hours signing up for a service. The whole process can be rather draining. Asking how long the process will take can help you set up another appointment. If, when you get there, the process takes much longer, feel free to tell the service that you have another appointment. This will also be a good barometer in telling you how a service treats its employees.

How Many Services Do I Need?

One of the unique things about temping today is the ability to have a relationship with more than one service. In effect, having more than one employer. In years past, temporary help services frowned on their employees accepting work from more than one service. But today, the competition is so fierce that services accept the likelihood that you will be getting work from other services. Sarah, who has been temping on and off for twenty years in New York, is registered with six services. "Right now I'm getting work from three of them. And they all know I'm working with other services."

Christina, who is registered with five services in California, found out that it can be a plus. "I let them know or let them suspect I'm signed up with other services and that seems to make them work much harder for me. If they like you and want to keep you, they will keep you working. In fact, I signed up with a service and the very next day they got me a job."

Doing The Service Shuffle

There is a big difference between being registered with a service and actually getting work from a service. While there is no upper limit to how many services you need, you should follow the steps outlined in this chapter to target the ones best suited to your needs. As you market yourself, you'll see that some services respond with work and others do not and will fall by the wayside. This is a natural process and you will be best advised to concentrate your efforts on those services that meet your needs.

In the long run, finding that one service that gives you the kind and amount of work you need is best. The advantages with working with just one service, of course, should be apparent: You will become known to them as well as to their clients, and you will have a greater chance of reaching the work hours necessary to obtain benefits. Unfortunately, you will probably have to deal with at least two services: your primary service and a second service that you can develop a relationship with and have a history with for those periods when your primary service can't find work for you. This will lead you into a dance I call the service shuffle.

The obvious downside of working with more than one service is the problem of navigating among them and keeping on the good side of all of them. Before Christina settled on that successful strategy, she made a mistake no temp should make. She was in the middle of a three-month assignment that she got from one service when she received a call from another service about an assignment that paid more. She quit her three-month assignment without notice. She got that other assignment with more money; she also never again got a call from the service she quit on. She now makes sure she lets the services know when she's on their schedule to avoid any unforeseen conflicts.

What happened to Laura, who used temping to earn extra cash while her husband went to law school, is a common problem that occurs when a person tries to maintain a similar relationship with one or more services simultaneously. "When I temped in New York City, I was just registered with one service and that seemed to work out just fine. But when my husband was accepted to a law school upstate, I registered with two and it didn't really work out. It just seemed that when one called and gave me an assignment, the other would call with an assignment for the same week and I would have to say no."

You can lose a service if you say no too often. When dealing with more than one service, make sure you keep communication open. If you've called a number of services and put yourself on all their availability lists, make sure to call the others back when you've gotten an assignment to take yourself off the availability list. This little extra effort will help keep your relationships with a number of services intact so that when you need them, they will be there for you.

Since services, like every business, can lose accounts and, therefore, become less reliable, the sign-up process is not a one-time event. You'll most likely find that you'll be signing up with services throughout your temping career. In the next chapter we'll discuss the sign-up process and how to really begin working with a new service so that you can move ahead of the competition and start making money.

Signing Up

When you first step into the office of a temporary help service to sign up, you are entering an increasingly competitive environment. The reason for this is there are more temps out there than ever before, and it's natural for personnel coordinators to call those temps who are proven assets first. As far as the service is concerned, you are the "new kid on the block" and, for a while, you should expect to be at the bottom of the list. You may think it's unfair that one temp will be getting 40–50 hours of work a week while you are getting 20; but you must understand that, as in any industry, you will have to prove yourself before you can be assured of the steady work and the type of work you want. Your arrival at the service to sign up is just the first step in the process. Let's take a look at the sign-up process and at how you can move up the list.

What Are Temp Help Services Looking For In You?

You can get off to a good start with a service by arriving on time for your appointment, dressing properly, and communicating your thoughts clearly and effectively. Yes, first impressions are important. Dress appropriately for the type of environment you expect to work in. That means if you expect to work in a corporation, you should wear what is normally acceptable in that environment. But even if you are seeking a job in an environment where dress codes are not required, or where you would be expected to wear a uniform, you should still wear good quality clothing that is pressed and clean, with polished shoes. Never go to sign up at a temporary help service dressed in jeans, a T-shirt, and sneakers.

I would dare say that a personnel coordinator will look more favorably upon an applicant with average test scores who dresses and communicates well than an applicant with excellent test scores who looks unkempt. Knowledge can always be gained by experience and a desire to learn, but appearance and the ability to communicate seem to say something about the inner qualities of a person.

The fact is, with the exception of schedule, temp help services look for the same things companies look for when hiring employees. After all, you will be working for a corporation. Robert A. Funk, chairman and CEO of Express Personnel Services, says, "We look for the same characteristics in our employees as do other employers, including reliability, punctuality, times or days of availability, good references from previous employers, and drug-free. With regard to skills, not only do we have all our applicants go through basic testing, but according to their area of interest, we have additional skills evaluations, as well as testing that may be necessary to meet a certain client's criteria."

You will also need to bring two forms of identification that prove you are either an American citizen or, if you are a citizen of another country, are legally allowed to work in the U.S. Any two of the following forms of identification are considered acceptable proof of your legal eligibility to work: a driver's license, birth certificate, Social Security card, proof of naturalized citizenship or, if you are from another country, a work visa. You should also take your résumé and the names and addresses of three past employers or, if your work history is thin, personal references.

The Visit

When you arrive, you will be given an employment application, reference cards, a skills questionnaire, and a W-4 form to fill out for tax purposes. If you have brought a résumé, be sure to tell the receptionist. Sometimes they will accept your résumé instead of making you fill out the application. Sometimes they still will make you fill out the application. No one said a temp service can't be bureaucratic!

Make sure you fill out all the forms. Some places have a lot of forms. Pay special attention to the skills questionnaire and check off all the skills in which you have experience. This will help the personnel coordinator determine what type of assignments you are eligible for. You will also be tested on those areas in which you want to work.

Testing

Once you have filled out all the forms you will be asked to take some tests. This will more than likely consume most of your time during the sign-up process. All applicants are asked to take a number of basic tests for grammar, spelling, filing, etc. Then, depending on the type of work you want to do, you will be asked to take some tests geared to that particular specialty to prove your proficiency. If, let's say, you want to test on a number of software packages, this will take additional time. The more tests you take, the better you will appear in the eyes of the service, especially if you do well on them. There is nothing like starting the interview with the words from the interviewer, "You've scored 100 percent on all your tests."

Even if you hate tests, there is really no reason to worry. Remember that you are not applying for a specific job, just the chance to get on the availability list. Even if you do not do that well, the service will always let you take the tests again, usually after a six-month waiting period. The fact of the matter is that many services use the exact same tests, especially the computer software evaluation tests. By the time you sign up for your third service, you will know all of the questions by heart and, hopefully, you will have researched the answers. Just take a positive approach and make the most of your time. The service is also interested in placing you on their availability list.

The Interview

The chances are good that the interview will come at the end of the sign-up process. You may be feeling a little frazzled by this time, having just filled out what seems like dozens of forms and taken a battery of tests, but cheer up—you are being interviewed because you did well on the tests. So just settle down, put a smile on your face, and greet the interviewer with a warm handshake. And remember that, unlike an interview for a permanent job where there is just one open position, your temp service interview is an open-ended discussion about your preferences and desires and how the service can meet them.

While the temp-service interview may be something entirely different than a job interview, it is still an interview. The way you present yourself, communicate, and answer questions, and the questions you ask all add up to determine if you are the type of person the service wants representing it. Remember that showing enthusiasm about the possibility of working as a temporary and being sure of your skills are important attributes to demonstrate during the interview. Just like any interview, you want to be positive about the future and show that you can be an asset to the company. If you go into the interview with a depressed attitude that says, "I'm going to be a temp; this is the end of the line for me," then you can be sure your career as a temporary worker will end before it gets started. The person who is interviewing you has been trained to spot all the verbal and nonverbal cues we use to communicate about ourselves. So, look sharp and be sharp.

All things considered, the temporary help service interview is not as stressful as an interview for a full-time position. Christina's experience is representative of the vast majority of people who have gone through it: "It's not bad," she says, "I never found it very stressful. They ask you what type of work you're looking for and you give a little bit of your background. That's a lot different than going in for a major job interview. And it's also a different feeling because a temp service is basically looking for people who are going to make them money. So it's kind of a two-way street, where a regular interview for a job is more highly stressful. With a temp service, as long as you have the skills, they are going to put you to work. Once you get that first assignment and you do a good job, they are going to call you back."

What Will I Be Asked? It might be helpful to have some idea of the kind of questions you'll be asked during the interview. Remember that the person who will be interviewing you is a trained professional who is not simply reading from a list of standard questions. Many of the questions will be based on the kind of information you supplied on the application. Nonetheless, there are some basic questions that most likely will come up in the interview. I asked Cheryl Ann Van Beek, customer service specialist for Norrell Corporation in New York City and a person who has been in employment services for seven years, what general questions she would ask an applicant. Here is what she said:

- If you've worked temporary before, how did you feel about it? Did you enjoy it, or not?
- If you've worked temporary before, what type of work did you usually do?
- Why did you leave your last place of employment?
- Why are you interested in doing temporary work?
- What type of environment do you feel most comfortable working in? Busy, or laid-back?

- What can you offer clients when you go out on assignment?

What Should I Answer: As you can see, there are no trick questions. The answers you give should be honest, direct, and brief, showing that you've already thought this through and you have an idea of what you want. Avoid long, rambling explanations of your goals or past. Make sure you show a positive attitude, especially when describing past temporary experiences. No one will want to send you out if all you have to say about temporary work is negative. If asked what you can offer clients, make sure you exude confidence and a "can do" attitude—even you if are short on skills. And if you are really interested in getting the best and highest paid assignments, make sure you tell your interviewer you like busy work environments. That shows you are ambitious, a go-getter, and willing to take on the tough tasks.

One of the major differences between the temp-service interview and a job interview is that the temp-service interview is much more reciprocal. Remember, as Christina notes, the temp service is looking for people who will make them money. They are not looking to eliminate you from a list of candidates, but to bring you in. Therefore, it's a much more comfortable experience than a job interview.

The other important difference, as Bob Funk states, is that the service is looking to find out when you are available and what you want. Most services operate under the principle that a happy worker is a productive worker, so a service will try to meet your criteria as much as possible. You can, therefore, make demands that you would never dream of making during a job interview. If you have any time constraints or preferences, you should make these plain during the interview.

What Should I Ask? Now is the time to go into greater detail about the service's fringe benefits, payment schedule, and salaries. Some of the questions you may wish to ask are listed below:

- If you are using temporary help as a bridge to full-time employment, ask if the service regularly places temps into full-time positions and what the procedures are, if any.

- If you have an industry preference, ask if the service has clients in the specific industry you want to work in. The interviewer will tell you if it does, but the chances are good you will not be able to find out if a particular company is one of the service's clients.

- Ask what the chances are of being kept busy for the amount of hours you want to work.

- Ask what salary ranges are for the kind of work you want to do.

- Ask about salary increases and/or seniority bonuses. Many services give increases based on performance and longevity. Note when and how these increases take effect. The chances are good you'll have to remind your service when you're due for a raise or bonus at the appropriate time.

- Ask about other bonuses the service may offer that will put money in your pocket. For example, many services give bonuses for referring other workers.

- Ask about stand-by programs and whether you get paid for them.

- Ask about the payment schedule and whether checks are drawn from a local or out-of-state bank. Checks drawn from out of state may take longer to clear. Some services have check cashing arrangements with local banks or have direct deposit. Ask about these services.

- Find out when your time card needs to be handed in to be processed for payment during the normal payroll cycle. Some services allow you to fax your time card to them, which certainly saves on a postage stamp or trip to the service to drop it off. But, remember, if you don't want a delay in getting paid, it is your responsibility to make sure your time card is at the service by the designated time.

- Ask about medical, hospitalization, and insurance plans and how you can become eligible.
- Ask about paid vacations and, once again, how you can become eligible.
- Ask about training and cross-training opportunities.

Your Impressions

Although you will be working in many different companies during the course of your temporary employment, you are an employee of the temporary help company. You should feel good about the temporary help company in general, and with your personnel coordinator in particular, and feel that the experience you just went through is the beginning of a productive working relationship. After you leave, you may want to personally assess the service to determine if it is right for you.

- Did you feel that the interviewer listened to your questions and answered them satisfactorily, or did you feel rushed?
- Did you feel that the interview was comprehensive and thorough?
- Did you feel that the interviewer was interested enough in you to learn about your skills, time availability, and experience?
- Did you get along well with the personnel coordinator? It is important that you feel you can work with her or him. This is the person who will be giving out the assignments so your success as a temp will, in a very real sense, depend on a good relationship. In addition, a good working relationship with your personnel coordinator can often offset that feeling of not being a part of the corporate environment you are working in.

- Do the proposed assignments seem interesting and an appropriate match for you? You will work better in environments you enjoy.
- Did you get an information packet?
- Did the interviewer give you his or her business card?
- Did the interviewer tell you when the usual call-in times are to put yourself on the availability list?
- Did the interviewer invite you to call if you had any questions about the service?
- Did they keep to the schedule?
- Are the phones busy? And if so, who's calling? Keep your ears open.
- Note how the company treats their regular temps who may walk in or call. If you have an opportunity to speak to any of them when you're on the premises, ask them about their experiences.

Getting on the "A" List

Now that you've signed up and have been evaluated, interviewed, and approved for hire by the service, you're ready to get right to work, right? All you have to do is sit by the phone and wait for it to ring, right? It can happen and it sometimes does. There are enough stories of people signing up with services and getting calls the very next day that the temporary industry's ability to do that has almost become mythic. Unfortunately, it doesn't usually work that way.

Although you are theoretically eligible for immediate assignments, the chances are good you won't be called right away. For one, the service will want to check your references before you are sent out. But a far more important reason is the fact that there are other temps out there with proven track records both at the service and at the service's customers. While they are known entities, you are just a name on the service's list at this point. It is up to you to make yourself into a person and to go from the new kid on the block to the service's "A" list.

While you can't compete with the temps with track records, you can compete with the other new temps. That will take some marketing. It's not as difficult as it sounds, but it is important to cut through the competition and to become more than just a name.

The day after you sign up, call your personnel coordinator and remind him or her that you were interviewed the day before. Thank him or her for taking the time and express your interest and desire to work as soon as possible. Always be courteous and professional over the phone. Ninety-nine percent of your dealings with your service will be via telephone and it's always important to be courteous and professional. These early contacts are crucial. You have now begun the process of making yourself a person and not just a name on a list.

Jack takes the idea of marketing very seriously, and it's one of the reasons why even in a city as large as New York, he is able to get the best assignments. "I would suggest following up with a new service daily until you get that first job. But I also do not hesitate to stop in and see them when I am in the area to discuss my skills again and the areas where I think I can be strong."

Remember when I said that flexibility is a two-edged sword? Well, getting that first assignment is one of those times when it's necessary to look at that other edge, the one with your name on it. Until you have proven yourself to the service, it may be necessary to be more flexible than you might otherwise wish to be. Here are some suggestions that may help you get your first assignment a little quicker:

- Accept an assignment for less money. When you signed up, you probably discussed not a set wage but a range of acceptable wages. Be willing to take an assignment that is at the lower end of your range. You should not, however, go below your bottom line or you may end up only being offered that rate in the future.

- Work on short notice. If your schedule permits, let your coordinator know you are willing to take assignments on short notice. That usually means you are called to work on the same day.

- Take an assignment outside your immediate geographical area.

- Take an assignment outside your immediate area of interest.
- Take assignments of any length. Perhaps you would prefer not taking assignments that last only a day or a week, but at the beginning, you would do well to take an assignment of any length. For one, the service will most likely want to test your on-the-job performance in shorter assignments and for another, the service's regular temps will have first call on the choice assignments.

Playing Matchmaker

When a customer calls the service for a temporary employee, the service gets the information it needs and then matches that information with an employee to find the best fit. The selection criteria services use are based on a number of factors, including the temporary employee's overall skill to fit the job, attitude, personality, distance from the job site, availability, and prior work history with the service (if any).

The chances are good that, whether the service is using some computer "match" program or is just going by a list, more than one person will fit the match. All things being equal, how does the personnel coordinator call you instead of the other person? This is where it comes down to the self-marketing that you are doing. It comes down to the human factor. When your personnel coordinator knows you because you have shown interest by calling, calling, calling, you have dramatically increased your chances of getting that call back.

The main thing to remember here is that you are trying to get your foot in the door. Flexibility and availability are the keys to unlocking that door.

If you've followed these steps, you've made a good start at having a successful temping experience. We'll take an in-depth look at how you can continue a productive relationship with your service in the next chapter. We'll also take a look at how to work with the other important part of being a successful temp—the client company.

The Temporary Help Service, The Client Company, and You

Becoming known at your service is just the beginning of the process. Just like any endeavor you get into, being successful involves some work. Being successful as a temp involves work on two fronts—the service and the client company. There are often complicated relationships between you and the service, the service and the client company, and, most importantly, you and the client company. The involvement of three parties is one of the major ways temping differs from full-time employment.

Your Twin Responsibilities

As a temp, you may sometimes feel that you are a David standing between two Goliaths. On the one side is your employer, the temporary help service. On the other side is the client company. In order to work, there are certain responsibilities you have to the service. In order to keep working, you have to play by the rules of the client. This is sometimes difficult. But if you know your responsibilities, you should have no trouble dealing with these two giants. And, you do remember what happened to the original Goliath, don't you?

You and Your Service

The first relationship you have is with your service. You started that relationship when you signed up and you will develop this relationship through continual contact and through the assignments you get. It's important to remember, first of all, that your service is your employer. According to a survey by the National Association of Temporary and Staffing Services, 33 percent of temporary workers don't realize that the service is their legal employer.

While it's true that the relationship between you and your service may seem unreal at times because you rarely see your personnel coordinator, if you forget who your employer **really** is, it may lead to other types of confusion. We have already looked at what the legal obligations of your temporary help service are to you, but an employer-employee relationship involves more than just legal issues. You, too, are a part of that equation, but if you don't remember that you are the service's employee, you can never meet your end of the bargain. That will be detrimental to your success as a temp. Let's take a few moments to see what your responsibilities are as an employee.

What It Means to be An Employee

Despite the nontraditional nature of your relationship with your service, you have a responsibility towards it, just like an employee in a traditional employment situation. Here are some examples of things that are not merely legal:

Loyalty: Your primary loyalty is to your service; it gets you the work. If you work for more than one service, loyalty, of necessity, must be divided among the group. But, in that case, you can't treat one better than another. At the very least, that means that once you accept an assignment from one service, you don't go back on your word if another service calls—even if the other assignment is more suitable. It is far better to turn down an assignment, then to say yes and then no.

Pride: Remember that the service you work for is a professional organization with highly skilled people taking care of the business side of things, and one with well-trained employees on location in major companies in your area doing productive and important work. Take pride in your own work as well as those out there who are also doing good work because, in a very real sense, what you do paves the way for other temps and vice versa. For example, when one of your co-temps does a good job at a company, it makes it easier for you to work at that company.

Confidentiality: Never discuss your service's other clients with clients and, if you work for more than one service, never, never discuss one service's clients with a personnel coordinator of another service.

Sense of Community: It's difficult to feel a sense of community with an employer you may rarely see and with co-workers you may never meet, but keep in mind that there are other employees working for that service and together, you form a community with a single purpose. The service companies can probably do a better job of fostering a sense of community among its employees by sponsoring get-togethers or picnics where all the employees can be assembled in one place and get to know each other.

Your Responsibilities As an Employee

In this sometimes confusing three-part relationship in which the service is your employer, but you are most often on location, your responsibilities will in some ways be similar and in others different from those of a "regular" employee. Rather than having few responsibilities, as you might expect, the more independent nature of temping places added responsibilities on you. The reasons for this are that there are no standard policies when it comes to rates, dress, etc. These policies change from company to company and from assignment to assignment. Your responsibilities include:

- Communicating your job preferences and time or travel constraints to your service at the beginning. Communication with your service on all levels can't be stressed enough.

- Completing an assignment once you accept it. Unless unforeseen and dire circumstances arise after you accept an assignment, you should make every effort to complete the assignment as it was described.

- Performing to the best of your ability as you would with any job.

- Making sure your time card contains the correct number of hours worked, is signed by the client company, and given to your service. Time cards must be handed in to the service by a specified time each week if you want to get paid on time. It's your responsibility to make sure it gets there and to know the payment schedule. Retain the employee copy of your time card so that you can verify that the amount on the check is for the correct number of hours at the correct rate of pay.

- Calling the service when your assignment is coming to an end, so that the service knows when you will be available for another assignment. You should also call if you want to take some time off to let them know you are not available.

- Letting your service know if you are asked to stay beyond the completion date of your assignment and how much longer you are expected to stay.

- Calling the service if you are asked to stay past your normal quitting time, as in working into what's normally defined the second shift. Most companies pay more for second shift, but some do not. You may not want to stay if your service is unwilling to negotiate a second shift rate differential (usually day rate plus one quarter of the rate) or the company will not pay the service for it. Note: some services will pay you the additional money out of their markup, but you must get an okay from your personnel coordinator.

- Calling the service if something seems wrong at the assignment location.

- Calling the service if you are sick or otherwise can't make it to the assignment. If it's not your first day and you have your supervisor's phone number at the company, you should call there as well. There can be a lag of as much as a half hour between your call to the service and the service's call to the company. Don't let the client company wonder where you are.

- Calling if you are involved in a work-related accident.

- Sharing job assignment feedback with your personnel coordinator.

- Making sure you let your service know if you change your address, phone number, or name.

- Being a goodwill ambassador. One of the additional responsibilities you have is representing your service when you are on assignment. People tend to judge the whole by the parts they see. If your performance is not up to par, it will reflect on the professionalism of your service, which, in turn, will put your service in a poor light. You have a responsibility to make sure your service looks good.

Your Service and the Client Company

In addition to the relationship your service has with you, a relationship also exists between your service and the client company. This relationship will probably not be with the person you are working for at the company but, at some corporate level, there is a person who has retained your service to provide temporary workers to that company.

Your service has had to make certain promises and commitments to the company. At the very least, these include a markup that is competitive with other services in the area. Perhaps a service will charge a little less to "get the account." Your service has also committed to providing quality temporaries, in the amount the company needs. I know of one case, for example, where the service promised that no more than 10 percent of their supplied temporaries will be unacceptable to the company. And in today's environment, temporary services go well beyond just supplying workers. Temporary help companies often train their temps on company-proprietary software or equipment, or are co-involved with company testing programs. Some large temporary services even train their client company's employees on new software programs.

As you can readily see, the relationship between your service and the client company is often complicated and involved, with lots of long-range commitments and promises. The temporary industry is a very competitive one. The pressure is on the service to keep those promises and commitments; if they don't, there's always another one out there that will. The service, in a real sense, has a divided loyalty. On the one hand, they need the client in order to make a profit; on the other, they need you to send to the client. This divided loyalty can be problematic for you if there is a problem at the client company, since there will always be many more temps than there are clients.

You and the Client Company

That brings us to your relationship with the client company. Making a great impression on your personnel coordinator is only half the job. No matter how well she thinks of you, she can only market you to the extent that a company is willing to try you. Despite talk of matching an employee's qualifications with the requirements of a client, there is also a human factor involved. The chances are good that the client company will have a number of temps that they call back again and again. I have known managers to go so far as to call a temp directly and ask that person to block off a certain period of time so that when they call the service and request that person, he or she will be "available." The reason why this happens is simple: They know these temps; these temps are proven entities. They don't know you and, until they do, it will be hit and miss. Some professions are harder to break into than others, such as the legal profession, and some companies are more reticent about bringing on new temps than others. Some companies are also beginning to take a more active role in choosing temporary workers, actually requiring interviews at the company for long-term assignments—just as if you were applying for a full-time position.

It is, of course, in the best interests of your service to get you work and you will certainly get your chance to prove yourself sooner, rather than later. When that chance comes, it is in your best interests to become a temp that a company can't live without. "I think the key to being successful at this business," says temp worker Jack, "is to develop a rapport with the client, so that when the client needs a temp, they think of you and when they call the service they ask for you by name. That's what's important and if a temp can get one or more client companies to think that way about him, then he's in good shape."

The first thing you must do is show that you can produce the work. As a temp, you will be required to catch on quickly without asking too many questions and to produce quality work under different conditions and situations. It may not be easy to come in from the outside, step into a situation, and produce as though you've been at the company for ten years, but that is oftentimes what is required.

The other thing you must do is show you can produce the work with a good attitude. Brian, for example, extends himself as much as he can. "I think the most important thing is to make the most of any situation and go out of your way. I never say no," he says. "If someone asked if I could stay a little late, I would say yes. Because that's the kind of people a company wants. The other thing is to respect the rules and the social atmosphere of the office. Every office is different. You have to do what the Romans do. And if you don't, they can easily say we are done with you. So, you have to just fit in. But once they got to rely on me, it's like they couldn't do without me."

Building a Positive Relationship with the Client Company

It's certainly nice to get to the point in your relationship with a client where they come to rely and depend on you. You can do this by first showing your ability and professionalism and by having a good attitude. Here are some other important ways:

- Arrive on time for the first day of your assignment and for every day of your assignment.
- Dress appropriately.
- Be a team player.
- Show ambition. When you complete a task, ask if there is other work to do.
- Don't take extended lunch periods, even if full-time co-workers do it.

- Don't make personal phone calls.

- Don't complain or make faces about tasks you are given. If problems develop, call your service. Don't air your complaints to the client.

- Don't take sides in an office dispute or get involved in office politics. Like a lover's quarrel, when both sides kiss and make up, they will both be mad at you for taking sides. Better to remain neutral.

- Don't gossip on the job or off. If you find out something about the company or an individual employee, don't spread it around. Keep the confidences that you are expected to.

- Respect work-related confidences. Temps get around and are often exposed to sensitive and confidential information. Let's say one day you work for a law firm that represents Defendant X, and the next you work for a law firm whose client is suing Defendant X. As you can see, loose talk may have serious consequences. Some companies require you to sign a Confidentiality Agreement, but even if they don't, keep in mind that the work you are doing belongs to the company you are assigned to.

- Respect the property of others. The chances are good that you'll be sitting at someone's desk. Don't rearrange that person's computer or filing system, or move their pictures of loved ones around.

- Expect respect in return. Don't think of yourself as "just" a temp—you are a skilled worker, capable of doing the job.

- Get good ratings on your evaluations.

Navigating the Corporate Hierarchy

Every company has a different corporate culture and a different way of treating its employees. Fortunately, as a temp, you can more or less steer clear of office politics. Still, it's important to remember that all companies have a structure. There is someone at the top of the structure and there is someone at the bottom of the structure. Unless your assignment is as the interim president, it's more likely you will find yourself closer to the bottom of the structure than the top. You shouldn't feel badly about that, or get upset about your position; that's just the way it is. Many temps think that just because they are temps they do not fit into the corporate hierarchy and, therefore, do not have to adhere to its structure. That type of thinking is completely wrong and will never get you that base of client companies so important to your success.

As Brian found out, applying yourself to the task at hand will put you in good with your coworkers. Don't ever show disgust if you are asked to perform tasks that are boring or routine or that you think are beneath you—this holds true whether you are asked to do a task by the senior vice president or by a support staff person. That support staff person, especially, can be important to you. Why? Because when it comes to calling a temp again, that support staff person can very easily say that you did not work out and someone else should be called. No matter how productive, sweet, and wonderful you've been to the professional staff, no supervisor is going to call a temp back if that department's support staff doesn't want that person back. So, when that support staff person asks you to do something that you'd like to turn your nose up at, it's in your best interests to do it. Remember, you can make that person an ally or an enemy. It's your choice to turn a situation to your advantage or not. So, learn how to navigate the corporate hierarchy—it's in your best interests to do so.

You Are Being Evaluated

Make no mistake about it, while you are working away, behind the scenes your performance is being rated and evaluated. These evaluations become part of your record and play an important role in getting the best assignments (not to mention continued assignments). All services will definitely call your supervisor to obtain an evaluation of your performance. In many cases, these are in writing. In addition to evaluations initiated by your service, many companies—especially those that use a lot of temps—have their own internal evaluation forms. They use these forms to determine which temps they will call back over and over again. Companies and services may rate you in the following categories:

- Technical skill
- Attitude
- Reliability
- Productivity
- Punctuality
- Attendance
- Appearance
- General behavior
- Ability to get along with others

Scoring consistently high on these evaluations will keep the assignments coming. Scoring consistently low will mean the phone stops ringing. No service can continue to place a person who keeps getting negative evaluations. It doesn't make good business sense. Rarely will a service tell you more than once that you've received a poor evaluation, especially if two poor evaluations come one after the other. It just stops calling. One of the realities of this three-part relationship is that your employer—the service—has not been a witness to your performance. That's why it's critical for you to develop a good general reputation and good rapport with your personnel coordinator.

All temps get an occasional poor evaluation; it's the nature of the business. The people you are assigned to don't know you, and it's possible you are having a bad day. We all have bad days, but the person evaluating you is not going to know you are having one. There are some people who are not going to be happy with your performance no matter what you do. They are probably not happy with anyone's performance. When your reputation is good with your service, the chances are equally good your side will be accepted and nothing more will come of it. However, once again, if something else should happen, you will probably not be called back.

If you want to make a go of it in this industry, it goes without saying that you should make sure your reputation for reliability and performance is impeccable. Because of the transient nature of the business and the veritable plethora of services, there may be a tendency to think that an individual can get away with a sloppy work ethic. It's a small world out there and bad news travels. Some companies use more than one service, so you'll never know when you'll run into that company again. Personnel coordinators change jobs, too, and you would not want that person to take word of your bad reputation along with them. In my own experience, I have regularly run into personnel coordinators at one service who I knew from another service, or employees at one company who knew me from a previous assignment at another company. It's much better, and profitable, if you make sure that people only have positive things to say about you, even though your assignment is only temporary.

Staying on the "A" List

Now that you have marketed yourself to the hilt by calling your service every day, and have built up a good rapport with your personnel coordinator, you must back up your words with actions. You must prove to that person that you are who you say you are. When you do, you will always get the best assignments. Here are four of the ways:

> **Be Flexible:** Ask a real estate agent what the three most important factors in buying property are and he or she will tell you location, location, location. Ask a temp, or anyone associated with the temporary worker industry, what the three most important qualities for temping successfully are and that person will tell you flexibility, flexibility, flexibility.

People looking at temping from the outside often associate flexibility from the temp's point of view and, to some extent, that's true. The temp lifestyle can enable you to gain as much control over your schedule as you need. But flexibility works both ways. If you want to remain on your service's "A" list, you won't say no too often. Turning down a few jobs in a row will definitely place you at the end of the list.

Don't Turn Down That Same-Day Assignment: A close cousin to flexibility is accepting the same-day assignment. Yvette Folk, a personnel counselor at Winston Staffing Services, Inc., a New York City-based temporary help company, can tell you how valuable doing this is for your marketability and success. "I run into a lot of cases where people don't want to work on same-day assignments because they feel it's not valuable to them. On the contrary, it is quite valuable. Working as a temporary employee is like building your own business. A lot of temporary help get requested back at assignments time and time again. So, in a sense, they are building up their own business as well. By being flexible and by being able to go out on what we call same-day assignments, that also helps a person build up that entourage of clients that will call them back. It also helps them in the way that sometimes an assignment that may be for one day can turn into a long-term assignment. Clients may use a one-day assignment as a way of seeing whether they can get a good employee they can keep on a continual basis."

It goes without saying that building up your client base is important to your success as a temp. Accepting a same-day assignment will also get you in good with your personnel coordinator. Being available is the cornerstone of temping. Keep some clothing ready for that unexpected call.

Pick Up Your Check: It might be easier to have your check mailed, but in a business where most of the activity takes place over the phone, it's good marketing to make sure you get to see your personnel coordinator from time to time, even if it's just to wave to him or her from a distance. Check day is an excellent time to do that. If at all possible, pick a time during the day when you know the service will not be busy to give you the opportunity to engage in a little "shop talk" with your coordinator.

Stick to Your Word: Once you have informed your service of your schedule, don't say no when the call comes. One sure way of getting dropped from the "A" list is turning down an assignment after you've told the service that you were available.

Maximize Your Earnings

There are many ways of making money in this industry once you've gotten on the "A" list. It's really just a matter of taking advantage of any opportunity that comes along. However, doing that is up to you. Here are a few examples:

- Stay in touch with your service. Just because your service is calling you does not mean you can relax and stop calling them. Never hesitate to call every day or, if the service has certain times to call, on those times to let them know you are available. If you are with a large service, don't just tell the receptionist you are available but ask for your coordinator. It's not the receptionist who gives out the assignments.

- Be extremely easy to reach by phone. The fact is that when a job comes in, the personnel coordinator has to fill the position as quickly as possible. It doesn't much matter whether you have worked your way up to the top of the list if he or she can't reach you. Consider getting call waiting on your phone, if it's available in your area. Don't want to be chained to the phone? Get a pager or even a cellular phone. These technological aids to communication have really come down in price and you will gain the undying respect of your personnel coordinator if he or she knows you have gone to this additional expense just to be available for work.

- Know your stuff. Don't be happy with just knowing the basics in your particular field, but go the extra mile to learn your subject thoroughly. If you know a word processing software application, for example, don't just know how to cut and paste. Learn about the other functions, such as merging and macros. The more you know, the more marketable you will be.

- Upgrade and expand your skills. Take advantage of your service's free skills program to learn new applications. Once you test on them, you will be eligible for assignments in those additional areas. If you see something, such as a computer program, at a client company that your service doesn't have on its system, don't hesitate to ask them to buy it so you can learn it. Services appreciate knowing what new areas of technology their clients are moving into. You will help them and help yourself, too.

- Ask for the highest paying assignments. Once you've gained confidence in your abilities, find out what the highest paying assignments are and go for them. Be persistent. You may have to be patient—when you go for another level, you'll be competing with other temps who already get those assignments.

- Work Overtime. Take every opportunity to put in extra hours. You are legally entitled to overtime pay—time and one half—in most states after working 40 hours in a week. Since you work for the temporary service, this does not mean working for one client only. If your total hours for the week are over 40, you will receive overtime from your service.

- Work on a standby basis. At the very least, tell your service that you will work on short—sometimes very short—notice. So, if you work in an environment that usually requires a suit, it means getting up and getting dressed and waiting by the phone, fully ready to leave when it rings. If you want to be more aggressive, you can take a trip to the service and sit in the waiting room. The advantage to this approach is that you are already there and the service doesn't have to make a million calls to find someone. This increases your chances of getting work considerably. Some services actually pay you, at a lower rate, to come in, have some coffee, and sit around for a couple of hours.

- Work holidays, evenings, and weekends.

- Make sure the good news travels. If you have received compliments for your work at a client company, ask your supervisor to pass them on to your service. Although services and companies do evaluate on-the-job performance, do not just rely on these formal, impersonal reviews. There's nothing like a call or a note to show your personnel coordinator that your work has been appreciated.

- Communicate with the client your own willingness to return to the company. Likewise, there's nothing like being called back to a client to put you in good stead with your personnel coordinator. But sometimes companies just call a temporary help service and ask for a temp. If you've particularly liked your assignment, make sure the person doing the calling knows your name and your willingness to return. The next time that person calls, you will be personally requested.

- Call the service a few days before your assignment ends to put yourself on the availability list.

Keeping Busy

If your primary or only source of income is temporary work, you will want to keep as busy as possible. Unfortunately, unless you are on a very long-term, indefinite assignment, there may be times when there's not enough work for you. These periods can come at any time and they can come suddenly. I often have been caught off-guard because they seem to come just after periods of great activity. I'll have been working 60-hour weeks, and then I'll have a week when I won't get a call. It's reasonable to say, well, "I've just worked all these hours and I can afford to take a week off," but all of a sudden three weeks go by and I still haven't gotten a call. Then panic starts to set in. It's important to recognize these slow periods and act quickly when they come. One thing to keep in mind is that it doesn't make any difference how much you've made in the past, it's what you're making now that counts.

Your success as a temp is largely in your hands. That's one of the beauties of temping. But you are also more dependent on the ups and downs of the market. When the slow periods come, as they most assuredly will, you can choose to be a victim or a victor. The ones who work steadily are the ones who rise to the challenge. When you encounter one of these periods, don't sit around waiting for the phone to ring. Be persistent and make those calls. You should:

- Call other services and let them know you are available for an immediate assignment. Different services often specialize in different industries, so when one industry is slow, another may be picking up.
- Take something that is not directly in your field, even if it's for less money. For example, if you are a word processor, take a secretarial position.
- Know the business cycles. Most industries have peak periods and slow periods. For example, office/clerical positions may slow down around the Christmas season while retail sales and product demonstration jobs will be on the upswing. Since the services themselves tend to specialize in one or a few areas, knowing which does what, when, will help you stay busy when your preferred industry goes into a down cycle. Of course, cycles also depend on the general economic climate and your geographical area.

Getting a Raise

Unlike working as a full-time employee in a corporation, temporary help services do not engage in annual reviews for the purpose of promoting you or giving you a salary increase. There are some services that give increases after you've worked for them for six months, but you can't count on them to automatically adjust your pay. As a temp, you will have to take on the responsibility of walking up to your personnel coordinator and asking for more money.

If you've worked steadily for a temp help service for more than six months, you should ask for an increase in wages. Your temp service will be more likely to say yes if you've had an excellent record with them. That means that you've gotten better than average evaluations, you are getting consistent call-backs from clients, and you've shown some initiative in upgrading your skills.

But there are also other occasions you may wish to ask for an increase in your hourly rate. Remember, you are in a competitive industry filled with numerous temporary help services who have many employees with varying skill levels. It's important to keep abreast of what is going on in the industry by finding out what other services are paying their employees for similar job functions with similar skills. If you find that another service is paying more for what you are doing, you should bring that up with your personnel coordinator. If they can't match the price, you should switch services. Loyalty can extend only so far.

You should also ask for an increase if your service calls you often for difficult assignments. That's a sure sign that you are getting excellent evaluations and you are becoming indispensable to your service. Perhaps you're pleased that the service is calling you frequently, but it's money that's the important thing, and when a service depends on you they are more likely to give you more of it. In this industry, sometimes you just can't be shy—you have to ask for what you think you deserve.

Trying to Outflank Your Service

Sooner or later in your temping career, the thought is going to cross your mind, "Hmm, why should the service make all this money off my labor, why don't I just cut them out and work directly for the company." Or, it may happen that a client will come to you and say, "I like your work, what if I pay you a little more than what you're getting and we'll cut out the middleman."

It might be tempting to be an independent temp, and there are opportunities to do just that. But doing it by trying to outflank your service is not the way to start your own little cottage industry. Besides being unethical, it is also illegal. If you read the back of your time sheet, you will see there is a prohibition against a client company using your services for a certain period of time, without paying the service a fee. Ignoring these contractual agreements may get you involved in a legal hassle. It will definitely result in the loss of that service as a source of income and give you a bad reputation.

Now that we've laid all the groundwork, it's time to jump right into an assignment. The next chapter looks into what you can expect during an actual assignment, including knowing when to ask for more money and how to deal with typical assignment situations.

8

The Assignment

The phone rings. It's your temporary help service with an assignment. There are four reasons your coordinator has called you:

- The length of the assignment matches your availability. (Remember you were the one who informed your service when you were available. To turn down an assignment at this point would not be a good move.)
- The job description given to your coordinator by the client company matches your skill level.
- Your personnel coordinator thinks you would be a good "fit" for the assignment.
- The pay scale is consistent with what you have informed the service you would accept for the type of work you are being asked to do.

Once you've built a good reputation with your service, there will be times when they will call you just because you're you. There will also be times when a client company will request you specifically. Those are gratifying times, for sure, but remember this is a business call.

Your coordinator is not calling to make small talk. She wants to give you all the particulars and move on to the next call. You want to make sure you have all the information you need to get to the assignment. Keep a pad and pen by the phone so you can write down all the necessary information. You don't want to have to call your coordinator back on the day of the assignment because you forgot to write down the address or the contact person at the client company.

This is the information your personnel coordinator should give you during the call:

- The start date
- The daily hours
- The expected length of the assignment
- The job description
- The pay rate
- The name and address of the company
- The person you will be reporting to at the company
- The dress code

If your coordinator hasn't given you all of this information, or you are unclear about any of it, now is the time to ask. Make sure you get the exact spelling of the company name and the contact person. If you are unsure about how to get to the assignment, ask for directions. You may also wish to ask what business the company is in.

It is important that you leave your coordinator with the feeling that she has called the right person. Always be positive when you are accepting an assignment and give off a "can do" attitude. This is especially important if this is your first assignment with that particular service. Even if you're a little rusty on something the personnel coordinator has told you will be part of the assignment, just say you can do it—and brush up on it later. Remember, being a temp is like being in business, sometimes you have to take a risk to move on to the next level. I'm sure you'll rise to the occasion. But, if an assignment comes along that is way above your skill level and you don't think you can handle it, then it's best to be honest and turn down the assignment rather than fail on the assignment.

And don't forget, in all cases, to thank your personnel coordinator for calling you.

Turning Down An Assignment

In a perfect world, all four of the match criteria will be met and you'll be off to an assignment. Unfortunately, we don't live in a perfect world. There will be times the service will call with an assignment that is below your pay scale or skill level, or when you aren't even on the schedule.

During those times you may find it hard to say no. Remember that it's okay to tell your service no when you don't feel an assignment is right for you. After all, flexibility is what temping is all about. On the other hand, don't make saying no a habit. If you turn down assignments too frequently, you will soon fall out of favor with the service. Services like their temporary workers to be available for assignments and when you say no too often, the service will just stop calling.

When you do have to turn down an assignment, make sure to do it in a way that tells the service you are still interested and to thank them for thinking of you. You can always say, "I would love to do that assignment, but I [have these tickets to a show/already told my mother I would have dinner with her/have friends visiting from out of town]. I'm sorry I can't do it but I'll be back on the schedule [tomorrow/on Monday/next week]." You get the idea.

If you come home one day and see the light blinking on your answering machine with a message from your service about an assignment you don't want to take, never, never fail to call the service back.

Negotiating for More Money

If you feel the pay scale is too low for you or too low for what the assignment calls for, you can do one of three things:

- Accept the pay as given.
- Turn down the assignment.
- Negotiate a better rate of pay.

Most temps think they must accept the pay scale as given or turn down the assignment; however, there are many times when a service will be willing to negotiate with you and you may be able to make 50 cents or a dollar more an hour. Personnel coordinators have the authority to make these decisions on the spot.

Negotiating for a better pay rate for an individual assignment is different than getting a general pay raise based on your length of employment with the service. This is something that you do at the time of the call and is only for the particular assignment being offered. Once you say yes to an assignment you are also saying yes to the rate of pay. The only exception to that is if you find, upon going to the assignment, that the job calls for a higher skill level than what you were informed. In that case, your service should pay you the competitive rate for the skills needed.

Other than that, though, there are definite times when you can negotiate for more money:

- If your personnel coordinator is asking you to do an assignment that is below your skill level and wants to pay you at the rate of the lower skilled position instead of at the rate you normally get. If a service can't fill a position, it may ask you to take a position that pays less than you normally get. When that happens, you can ask to be compensated at your usual rate and oftentimes, the service will accommodate your request.
- If you know that another service is paying more for a similar job description.

- If you feel the assignment is particularly complicated or involves specialized knowledge.

Negotiation is an art; it must be done tactfully. There are plenty of books on the market that deal with the subject of negotiation—this is not one of them. This section is here to let you know that you do not have to accept the pay rate without question and that there is some negotiating room. Newcomers to the field should not try to negotiate a higher rate of pay; however, this does not mean you should go below the bottom line figure you discussed with your personnel coordinator at the interview. As you become more experienced and relied on by your service, you will be in a better position to get more money for individual assignments as they come your way. Remember, if you don't ask, you'll never know.

Keep in mind that the service is marking up your hourly wage to the client and within that markup is the raise that you will get after six months. You don't think the service suddenly charges the client more for you just because it's given you a raise, do you? Of course not. The raise has been in there all along. When you negotiate for more money, what you are negotiating against is the service company's profit margin. When you get a raise, the service company is saying, in effect, it is willing to make less money on you than on someone else. Admittedly, there is a negotiating limit, but when you become a key player at the service company, it increases your negotiating power and the company will be willing to make less on you per hour.

As a case in point, I was requested by a client company to work a 9 p.m. to 9 a.m. assignment two days a week every week. I was not interested in taking public transportation at that time of night, but the company would not pay for car service because it fell outside its guidelines for company-paid rides. My service, however, wanted the business and offered to pay for the car, an amount equal to 25 dollars. It happened that after a few weeks, the company changed my schedule so that I was working from 12 p.m. to 12 a.m., which gave me a company-paid car home. Knowing that my service was now going to save the 25 dollars (or approximately $2.00 per hour), I negotiated a raise. We split the difference, giving me an extra dollar an hour and saving the service a dollar. We were both happy, and that should be the result of any good negotiation.

Dressing for Success

Some temps, unfortunately, feel that just because they are temps, they don't have to dress in a manner consistent with the company they are assigned to. That attitude will quickly remove that person from the service's call list. As a temp, you are responsible to follow all the procedures of the client company, including its dress code. As a temporary worker, you are not only the employee of the service but, to a very real extent, its image. You are, in most cases, the only contact with the service the client company's employees will see and the way you look and act reflects directly upon you as well as your temporary help service. If you do not look professional, your service will not look professional. And when your service does not look professional, the client company will call another service that does. Appearance does count—big time!

Your personnel coordinator mentioned the dress code to you during the call—corporate, casual, dress down. If you are not sure of the specifics, ask, but here are some useful guidelines:

> **Corporate:** Women should wear a dress, a suit, or a business skirt or dress pants with a nice blouse. Flats or heels are acceptable. Men should wear a conservative-colored suit (if you have one) or a sports jacket and dress pants. A button-down shirt and tie is definitely required. Polished loafers or lace-up dress shoes should be worn. If you are a man with long hair, your hair should be neatly combed and tied back.

Many people wear running shoes to work and then change into dress shoes once they get there. This might be acceptable, but on the first day, it is better to wear the shoes you will be wearing in the office.

Casual: An informal blouse and skirt for women or casual slacks or nice jeans for women and men. A sport shirt, with no tie, is acceptable. This, of course, does not include "fashionably" torn jeans.

Dress Down: You can probably wear just about anything. Nonetheless, your clothes should be clean and pressed.

In general, it is always advisable to look better than worse on the first day. Even corporations that have strict dress codes may relax these codes for employees in some departments—for example, the mail room or the word processing center. Once you're at the job site, you can see how the full-time employees in that department dress and adjust what you're wearing accordingly on following days.

There are also certain times of the year, or certain days, when companies allow employees to wear more casual clothing. Your personnel coordinator is most likely unaware of these details and will give you a dress code based on his or her general knowledge.

During the week between Christmas and New Year's one year, I was assigned to a major investment banking firm where the dress code was not only corporate but as conservative as you could get without the feeling you were dressing for a funeral. You can imagine my chagrin when I walked into the place, garbed in my Sunday best, and saw everyone dressed down.

The next day, I walked up to a vice president and said, "How come you're a vice president and you're dressed in jeans and I'm a temp wearing a suit?" To that he laughed and said it was because of the time of year and suggested that I speak to my contact person at the company.

Unfortunately, she couldn't give me permission to dress casually because she needed to ask her boss who was on vacation. But she couldn't really say no because every one else was dressed casually. A real bureaucratic Catch-22.

I asked her if she would fire me if I dressed casually for the rest of the week. No, she said, she couldn't do that either. So I made an executive decision and dressed casually the next day and for the rest of the assignment, which made me one happy camper. However, I also informed my service of the situation.

You don't have to call your service over every little thing, but it's a good idea to keep them informed when changes on the job may affect your ability to perform or may have political consequences. In this small matter of wearing a suit versus casual clothes during the holiday week, I was not able to get a direct yes to my question. I could not be certain, when I came in the next day, that no one would have a problem with the way I was dressed. By informing my service beforehand, I equipped them to handle a possible complaint, and made sure I was covered.

Assignment Length

Assignments can vary from less than a day to many months to a year or longer. In general, as corporations rely more heavily on temporary workers, assignments have gotten longer.

When your coordinator tells you how long an assignment will last, he or she is giving you an approximate length, based on what the client company told him or her. Other than the four-hour minimum charge that most services charge their clients, there are no guarantees that an assignment will last as long, or as short, as the originally stated length. If you have followed the advice on how to select a temporary help service, then you are signed up with a reputable company that has reputable clients. Their word will be their bond and you will be able to count on what they say. Of course, no one can predict the future and things beyond anyone's control can happen.

You can help yourself determine the length of an assignment by asking exactly what the position is. If you are replacing a sick or vacationing employee, for example, you will know that as soon as that employee returns, your assignment will end. These assignments last anywhere from a day to a maximum of three weeks. If you are replacing an employee who is on maternity leave or disability, then you can be certain of a longer-term assignment, but one that has a definite end to it. Longer-term assignments also include ones in which the company is interviewing for a replacement to fill that spot or the company is testing a position to see if it needs a full-time employee. In most cases, your personnel coordinator will know the particulars about the position, but if he or she doesn't, ask when you get to the job.

In today's corporate environment, companies designate certain positions to be filled only by temporary employees. These positions have no specific ending date and are of indeterminate length. They are mostly project-oriented positions, which means they will last until the project ends. I once was on a project that was supposed to be completed in three weeks but instead, lasted for six months—it just kept getting bigger and bigger and bigger.

While there are no guarantees, your commitment to the service is what is critical when asking about job length. If you are informed that an assignment will last two weeks and you take it, it is up to you to complete it. Your word must be your bond. When a service knows it can depend on you, it will treat you with respect. If a job ends sooner than expected, a good service will put you at the very top of their list and get you work right away because they know you were depending on the income they said you would make from that assignment. When a job lasts longer than originally planned, feel free to ask the service to find a replacement for you if your schedule won't permit you to complete the extended assignment. You should, however, give the service a few days notice so they can find an adequate replacement.

Reporting to Work

Meeting new people and getting involved in new situations can be exciting and exhilarating. It can also be stressful. Even if you're a seasoned temp and you've had hundreds of first days, they can still produce anxiety. If you've had some notice, figure out what you're going to wear the night before the assignment starts, so you don't have to worry about it in the morning, and get a good night's sleep. I try to feel confident about my ability. If I'm sure I can do the job, that makes me feel better; it also makes the people I am about to meet feel better. When I'm going into a situation where my skills have become a little rusty (especially if I've told my personnel coordinator that I'm an expert at something I haven't done in two years), I pull out a book the night before and go over the important points of, let's say, a software program.

Besides being well groomed, try to get to the assignment at least fifteen minutes before you're supposed to start work so that you can familiarize yourself with the environment and equipment.

When you first walk into the company, introduce yourself to the receptionist by stating your name, the fact that you are there to work as a temporary worker, the temporary help service company you are from, and the name of the person you are reporting to. Your assignment starts the moment you walk in the door and the receptionist says, "May I help you?"—not when you meet the person you are working with. It is important to act professionally and courteously to every one you meet. First impressions last. Be confident, smile, shake hands, and establish eye contact. These simple actions will get you off to a good start. Remember, while it's the first day for you, it's also the first day for them.

I would like to say that the person you are to report to will give you the grand tour of the company, introduce you to everybody you need to know, explain in detail everything you are supposed to do and, in general, make you feel like you've been working there all your life.

Unfortunately, that is not always the case. Some people do, while some people throw work at you even before you sit down. Whether or not the company rolls out the red carpet for you is probably a product of the part of the country you are in, whether the company is large or small, or whether the person you are dealing with is having a bad day or not. Remember, you are there to do a job and it's up to you to do it well.

Once you are settled in, call your personnel coordinator at your service to let him or her know you are there and how the situation "feels" to you. In temp jargon, this is called posting in. Most services require that you do call within a reasonable period of time on the first day of a new assignment; some do not. Whether they do or don't, though, it's a good idea to do it anyway.

Bring Your Own Paper Clips?

I was once waiting in the reception area for the contact person to bring me to my assignment when I struck up a conversation with the receptionist. It turned out she was also a temp. She was a woman in her mid-fifties who had been temping for about fifteen years. We began talking about some of the little annoyances of temping, like not knowing where anything is. "Oh," she said, picking up a pair of scissors, "that's why I always bring supplies with me. I bring scissors, a ruler, a stapler, and paper clips. My husband can't understand why I bring these things in when the company is supposed to have them but, it sure makes my life simpler."

Obviously, her husband never temped. While I wouldn't go quite that far, I sure could sympathize with her sentiment. It's the little things that make temping so difficult. People, places, and things that full-time employees know without thinking can be extremely disconcerting to a temp. And, like I said, you can't always depend on the contact person to show you where everything is and who everyone is.

The First Day

The first day of any new assignment can be especially frustrating because there's no way for you to know all the little things (like where the paper clips are) that full-time employees take for granted. But with a little foresight and planning you'll be able to make the first day, and all subsequent days, go a lot smoother. Listed below are some pointers culled from temps with years of experience in dealing with unfamiliar situations:

- On the first day of your assignment get in a little earlier. Do a quick check around your desk. Perhaps the person you are replacing has left you a note explaining the setup.

- Look for and locate supplies you think you'll need beforehand.

- Find out where fax machines, photocopy machines, the supply room, rest rooms, and fire exits are located.

- Ask the person or persons you are working for if they answer their own phone, or do they expect you to answer it for them and, if so, how.

- Get a little Post-it® pad and write the names of everyone you are supposed to answer the phone for and stick their names next to their extension numbers on your phone.

- Find out the extension number of the receptionist and how to transfer calls and put callers into voicemail.

- If it's a large company, most definitely look for the company directory.

- If you will be using a computer network, make sure you know how to log on to the network and how the network file management system works. If you're in a large company, get the extension number for the Management/Information Systems department, or the User Support group.

- Be friendly and courteous. Introduce yourself to coworkers, if you haven't already been introduced to them, and let them know why you are there and how long you expect to stay.

- Be confident. Even though it's your first day, show people you are ready, willing and able to do the job.
- If you have any other questions, ask. It is often a lot easier to find out information at the beginning of the day before you get busy or co-workers get busy. They may not have time for you later. They especially won't have time for you a few days later if you're asking the same basic questions. It's best to get all the fundamentals out of the way sooner than later.

More Than a First Day

Unless your assignment is only for one day, you'll be back the next morning, feeling more self-assured and ready to handle the continuing tasks of your job. Now the focus begins to switch from getting to know where things are and how things work to your actual job performance. It's important to keep in mind that just because you are there only on a temporary basis, this does not relieve you of the responsibility of acting professionally and in accordance with established office practices. There is not just the fact that your performance will be evaluated by the client company and reported to your service, but, more importantly, you are a member of a team who is depended on by other members. In any work situation, your ability to communicate and establish rapport with co-workers and supervisors alike is essential.

Here are some pointers to help you maintain good relations and have a productive assignment. Although many of them may seem basic, it's amazing how many temps seem to forget about them, simply because they figure they will only be there a short time.

- Be a team player. Always be ready to lend a hand to any project that comes up and always ask if anyone needs any help if you aren't busy at the moment. It will be appreciated and will get you remembered the next time someone in that department needs a temp.

- Use simple pleasantries in your dealings with others. Say things like good morning, please, and thank you.

- Inform people of your skills and ability to do the job. I once sat, doing absolutely nothing, for three days because my supervisor had assumed I was just there to answer her phone and was giving her word processing work to the other secretaries.

- Communicate daily with supervisors on the status and progress of projects.

- Tell co-workers when you are going out to lunch or will be away from your desk for an extended period of time. This is especially important if your job requires answering phones.

- If you are using a computer and files may be difficult to locate after your assignment is over, keep a list of documents which includes the creation date, subject matter, and file and path name.

- Call both your temporary help service and your immediate supervisor at the client company when you are sick.

- Inform both your supervisor and your service a few days ahead of time if you need to take time off for personal business. Ask your service to call the client to see if they need a replacement for you. Do not leave this up to the client. Some companies use more than one service and they may call another service, resulting in a loss of income for your employer. Remind everyone again the day before.

- If your assignment is long term, check in with your service on a regular basis to remind them that you are still there and the status of your job. Be sure to call them immediately if your assignment changes from its original description.

- If you are looking for a full-time position at the client company, inform your supervisor and ask if you can submit a résumé. But before you do that, read chapter 9 on getting a full-time job through temping for more information.

- If you need to leave an assignment before its scheduled completion date, inform your service and the client a few days ahead of time. If the reason why you are leaving is because some work-related problem has developed, call your service before you decide to leave. They may be able to solve the problem. If the problem is unsolvable, you should still try to finish out the day.

Last Days

Ah, those last days. The one thing that's certain about being a temporary worker is that the day will come when it's time to say good-bye. The last day is very much like the first in that you want to start with a good impression of yourself and you want to leave a good impression behind. Here are some things to keep in mind on those hectic last days:

- Never leave a job on a bad note. Even if a job has not been particularly pleasant—and there will be assignments like that—it is important to try to leave a job in a positive way. If your service hears from a couple of clients that you have a habit of leaving a job badly, the service will stop calling you. Don't burn any bridges. If, for some reason, you've had to terminate an assignment due to unpleasant circumstances, it's not necessary to bad mouth the company or its employees before you leave. Just walk out with your dignity intact. There will be very few, if any, assignments of this nature.

- Make sure to take any personal items of yours with you when you leave.

- Leave your work area neat, clean, and orderly for the next person. If any mail or other material has come in for the returning full-time employee, put that in plain view.

- Make sure that the person's desk you have been using is in the exact same condition that you found it in, with his or her photos and personal items undisturbed.

- Write a brief note to the returning employee or inform your supervisor about the status of all projects you've been working on.

- Inform co-workers you are leaving.

- Although your time sheet has been signed on a weekly basis, the last day of an assignment is the time when you most likely may forget to get it signed. Make sure you keep it in view so you won't forget. Keep the employee copy for your records.

- Make sure you thank your supervisor for the opportunity of working there. A brief note of thanks with your name and your service on it may help remind that person to think of you the next time a temp is needed.

- Call your temporary employment service to remind them that this is your last day and put yourself on the available list.

Ice Breakers

It's difficult to walk into a new situation on a regular basis. While some temps thrive on it, others put a wall between themselves and the people on the job. It's an awkward time at best. Who should break the ice? You or the full-timer? Don't stand on ceremony.

While your approach to any job situation should be one of professionalism, appearing friendly and easy to get along with is an essential ingredient to successful temping. Not only will it make your assignment more pleasant, it will help get you that important call-back. People don't want someone in their office who is sour and dour.

Be pleasant and polite. Let people know by your attitude that you like being there. If necessary, assure them you are not after their job. And, remember, people like talking about themselves and their jobs. Asking people about how long they have been working there and some generic job talk is an easy conversation starter. But don't prattle on about yourself and don't interrupt busy people with idle chatter.

Some Typical Office Situations

One of the pluses of temping is the variety of assignments and environments, so there really is no such thing as a typical office situation.

But there are some general situations that may come up more than once in your temping experience. We'll take a look at these below.

This Job Description Doesn't Match

Your personnel coordinator told you the kind of job you will be required to do and you go to the firm and that's what you do. Right? Not always. Your personnel coordinator is just relating the information he or she received from the client company—and sometimes that information is just plain inaccurate.

In the vast majority of cases, the actual job will fall within a certain range of skills that met the description you were given. One of the most common complaints of companies is that they get temporary workers who are not up to the skill level they want. I suspect, therefore, that some companies intentionally bump up the description on the theory that if they request someone who can do more than is really needed, they will be getting a higher quality employee. If I had a nickel for each time my personnel coordinator told me that the company was looking for a highly skilled word processor when, in fact, they were looking for someone who could do photocopying, I would have been able to retire a long time ago.

When this happens, it really is your call on what to do. When the company has bumped up the description, they also realize they are paying more for someone who is doing less. Some temps are satisfied to be getting the wage of a word processor and doing general clerk work. Personally, I don't like being bored and I will call the service and say, "Hey, this company asked for a word processor and what they really need is a general clerk. Can you please find me a replacement?" I do believe most services appreciate this. Why? First, because they don't want to waste your abilities on something someone with less skills is capable of doing, and, second, they do want to keep you happy.

On other occasions, a job may require more skills than the description you received. In that case, if you have the skills to do the job, you probably should be getting paid more. Call the service and explain the situation. They will need to speak to the client and arrange a higher billing rate. If the service appears unwilling to do that, I would not work for that service again.

On very rare occasions the job description is nothing at all like the actual job. I heard of one case where a company asked for ten temps to do general office work. When the temps got there, they were shipped to a warehouse for a picking and packing operation. In that situation, the service called all its temps back and fired the client.

I'm Working for the Whole Gang

There will be many times when you will be working for more than one person. With the advent of computers and downsizing, even full-time support staff find themselves working for two, three, or more people at the same time. Maintaining your cool and getting the work out in these situations is really an exercise in prioritizing and communicating.

First, prioritize the work in order of importance and timing. In most corporations, importance usually depends on the level of the individual you are working for. So, if you are working for a senior vice president and a vice president, the senior vice president's work takes precedence, even if it really isn't more important. That's just the way the game is played. Still, it's important to communicate to all what is going on— this will avoid conflicts later on. It would be helpful to tell the vice president that you'd like to get his work out, but you just got this urgent assignment from the senior v.p. If the vice president thinks his work is more important, let him speak to his boss about what you should do. In other words, let them fight it out between themselves.

There Is Absolutely Nothing to Do

There are situations when you have to hit the ground running and are expected to know what's going on as if you've been there for ten years.

There will be other times when you'll have absolutely nothing to do and you'll be asking yourself why they even need a temp here. Sometimes temping means sitting there and doing nothing. Sometimes it's because some big shot's secretary is out sick and that person wants a warm body sitting there to answer the three calls he or she is likely to get that day. Sometimes a company will want you there just in case something comes up. Or sometimes, something was expected to have happened but just didn't.

If there really is nothing to do, you are always free to call the service and ask them to get you out of there. But before you do that, you may want to explore some other avenues.

You can politely remind your supervisor that you exist and are capable. Sadly, some people think you just don't know how to do anything, so they don't give you anything to do.

If your supervisor doesn't have anything for you to do, ask one of the other support staff members in your department if there is anything you can help with, making sure you inform them that your supervisor doesn't have anything for you at the moment. Other support staff often will appreciate your help and initiative. But it's also likely that even if they are busy, they will be unable to give you anything to do because they will be doing something that you just couldn't do, like figuring out travel vouchers. If that's the case and no one seems to mind that you're not doing anything, avail yourself of an opportunity to learn something new.

The computer sitting on your desk contains a wealth of information in the form of software packages. Take the opportunity to learn a program you may not be familiar with or get a more in-depth view of a program that you are already know. It's been said before, but it's worth saying again, the more you know about computers, the greater your chances of finding work at a good rate of pay. Take every opportunity to learn. Read the company literature. This can be a great idea, especially if you are in the job market. And the more you know about a company, the greater your chances of finding full-time employment will be. And, when all else fails, you can always read a good book or play computer games.

When things are slow, don't spend your time making personal phone calls or making a nuisance of yourself by talking to busy co-workers.

I Can't Stand This Assignment

Believe it or not, there will be assignments you just can't stand, for whatever reason. If you are in such a situation, call your service immediately and tell them you want to be replaced. More than likely they will ask you to remain at the assignment until they find a replacement. Usually, that means the end of the day. But, if it's more than one day, stick it out. Remember, you are working for the service. If you leave suddenly, you will not get another assignment from them.

They Are Treating Me Like an Idiot

Some people have just not caught up with present day temp workers. They may think we are temps because we can't get a job. It might not dawn on them that we can't get a job because there are no jobs to get or because we have something else we want to do with our time. Consequently, we run into people now and then who think they have to explain the simplest things. If that should happen to you, it's all right to inform the individual in a polite manner that you are already familiar with the task and you can handle it. That person may actually be grateful a long explanation isn't necessary.

They Are Acting Like Idiots

It's bad enough that you have no idea how to do things, though at least you have an excuse. But when the full-timers don't know how to get something done, it can be frustrating. It's amazing how often I've been asked to do something by my supervisor only to find out that there's no one to help me. The reason? The person I'm replacing is the only one who knows how to do it. Who knows where that full-timer hid those files on the directory? When you're in a situation like that, don't get frustrated, just try to muddle through. It's times like this that it's good to have a personnel coordinator you can call and just vent to.

Office Politics

Many temps see temping as a way to stay away from office politics. While temping gives you some freedom from office politics, it does not make you immune. I suppose if you wanted to get away from politics completely, you would have to move to a deserted island. Politics are about people, and as long as there are people there will be politics.

It seems like no matter what you try to do, you will find people who are intent on getting you involved in the interplay of personalities in the office. While you can't control the actions of your coworkers, you can control your own behavior. It's in your own best interests to stay away from office politics as much as possible. Never take sides in an office dispute. Never repeat information about other people. In short, mind your own business.

Competitive Coworkers

Full-time employees can be a notoriously insecure group these days. Even if their company hasn't experienced downsizing, they are well aware that it is happening. The idea that the company may replace them with you or that you may want their job is not uncommon. Consequently, one of the things temps deal with is trying to convince the full-time staffers that they don't want the job—even if they do.

When jealousy and resentment rear their ugly heads at the workplace and are directed at you, it can certainly make for an unpleasant experience. "In some cases you're looked upon as a threat because people are afraid for their jobs," says Sarah, who has found a way of disarming people so that she can do her job without also having to deal with resentment. "If you're very good, they don't like that, and if you're not good, they don't like that either. It can be very difficult, and you have to be very careful. What I do is make them know immediately that I don't want the job by saying I'm interested in going into a different industry. And that helps."

Being Made to Feel Like an Outsider

Even if co-workers are not jealous of you or concerned about their jobs, they may not readily accept you into their fold. The reason is simple: They don't know you. Because of this, they may not trust you, or they might feel you don't have the same stake in your work as they do, or maybe they just don't want to expend energy on getting to know someone who will soon leave. Whatever the reason, being made to feel like an outsider by others, when you probably already feel like one, can make an assignment an unpleasant situation. After all, these are the people you will be spending a great deal of your time with. As a temp, you may experience this type of attitude on an assignment. This seems to be natural and soon resolves itself as people begin to feel more comfortable with you. If it doesn't, you should check out your own attitude. Perhaps you have put up an invisible wall around yourself that is keeping people out. Remember, you also have to extend yourself to co-workers and make them feel comfortable around you.

Just Dealing with People

As you can see, temping is really just as much about dealing with people as it is about producing. If you get your work done and maintain a low profile, you'll find that most situations can be successful and productive. By and large, people are not so bad to deal with. And those that are difficult are usually under a lot of stress themselves. Many times temps are called into situations that are critical before they get there, so the elements that produce stress already exist.

If you overhear your supervisor say, "I can't wait for my secretary to get back," it can make you feel pretty bad. But you have to bear in mind the person you are replacing has been doing the same job possibly for years and you cannot hope to know everything the regular secretary does. You sometimes have to realize that an insensitive remark is not really directed at you personally, just at the situation.

When someone is overbearing or demanding, it's possible the person is under some incredible deadline pressures. I've worked with investment bankers who haven't slept for days, trying to get out a proposal. They can get mighty grumpy. If a coworker is terribly uncooperative, maybe that person is jealous. Jealous of the fact that you may want a job, or just jealous that you can walk away from the company anytime you want. Ultimately, it should make no difference to you. You are there to do a job and that's your concern.

If you can be proud of the work you do and know that, at the end of the assignment, you've done the best job you were able to, that's what counts.

Temping at Law Firms

In the office/clerical/word processing end of this industry, getting assignments at law firms is one of the most lucrative areas. It is also one of the hardest and most difficult fields to break into. So, I suppose it's no coincidence that it pays so well. Lawyers, on the whole, expect a lot from their support staff, and temps are no exception to the rule. You'll find pressures and demands placed on you that don't exist in many other assignments. There is also the matter of understanding something about how to set up legal court documentation and having some basic understanding of legal terminology. Most law firms also use client/matter codes for everything that is done, including codes for making just one photocopy. Just trying to find those pesky codes somewhere in some client/matter book can be time-consuming—and don't expect the attorney to help you; he or she just wants the work done. But, if you are interested in making good money at temping, legal word processing is it. If you can get a good reputation in this area, you'll never have trouble making money.

Evening/Night Work

Like temping in the legal field, working evenings and nights should be one of the areas to strive for, especially if you live in a geographical area where companies have second and third shifts and if your schedule permits it. Why? Because it pays the best. However, there are also other benefits to working evenings and nights. Dress codes are more relaxed and night people, in general, seem more laid-back and less concerned with office politics and game playing. Perhaps this is because they are removed from the daily activity and gossip that takes place during the day. These shifts require some specialized knowledge and are usually reserved for the best temps.

I See a Better Way

As a temp, you may find yourself in a situation where you believe you know a better way of doing something the company is doing. This is not as unusual as it sounds. Temps have wide exposure to many different office environments and can judge from their experience what works best. Temps can also be objective and can see things that those too involved in a project sometimes miss.

I once worked in the Trusts and Estates department of a major law firm on what originally was a three-week assignment, but became indefinite due to an unexpected illness of the person I was replacing. I noticed that the boilerplate material used for the wills was placed on the computer in an inefficient manner. Just to make my job easier, I began to organize it and automate it so I could do the job a little faster. Some of the attorneys got word of what I was doing and took an interest in the way I could do it. Soon, what started as something that was intended to make my job easier became a priority project for the whole department. Attorneys worked feverishly to update the boilerplate material and I automated the entire process, reducing the average time of creating a basic will from two hours to fifteen minutes. Everyone was happy with the results, except my service. Why? Because my service said I should have been getting paid a much higher rate for doing what amounted to programming.

What I should have done was notify my service first. And that's what you should do. In my case, my ideas were well received and the money aside, everything worked out fine. Unfortunately, not all companies are receptive to new procedures, even when they can save time and money. So, if you see a better way of doing something, don't do what I did—notify your service and tell them of your ideas. They will be able to pass the information on to the right people, possibly giving you a nice pay increase in the process.

National Temporary Help Week

It's a common myth that temps do not get appreciated for what they do. However, that hasn't been my experience or the experience of other temps I've spoken with through the years. If anything, the opposite is true. More often, we seem to get more appreciation from supervisors than permanent employees. Maybe we receive appreciation because people expect so little of us and whatever we do looks like a bonus, but I don't believe that to be the case. Temps are so commonplace in the corporate environment that most people have come to understand what a difficult job temping is. It's certainly not easy going into a new place and producing like you've been there all your life. Yet, each day, that's what temps do. And, for that, we are indeed appreciated. You might be interested to learn that the United States Congress appreciates temps. It has declared one week in October "National Temporary Help Week."

What Really Counts

Ultimately, a temp is there to do a job, not necessarily to be liked or appreciated. If the work gets done well, we get the respect that should be accorded to any individual who does a good job. "I think a mistake a lot of people make is that they want to automatically be liked," says Christina. "To me, being liked is not nearly as important as being respected. If I'm doing the best job I can, people are going to respect me for that. If I go in respecting other people, not hoping to be liked necessarily, but to be a coworker and to do my job, just like they are there to do their jobs, I think the other things come along naturally."

And when you've done the job and your assignment is over, your service will thank you by giving you another assignment. Now that's respect and appreciation.

When to Say No

Temporary services have strict guidelines concerning what their employees are not responsible for at the client company. These are usually printed on the back of your time card and include not being entrusted with unattended premises, cash, negotiables, or other valuables. There usually is also a prohibition against operating machinery or motor vehicles without the prior written consent of the service. This is to protect the service, and you, from any possible legal hassles. If you are asked to do anything that is expressly prohibited by your service, you should definitely say no.

In addition to those things listed on your time sheet, you should say no if you are asked to do anything of questionable legality or that may jeopardize your health or finances. These include:

- Working in a hazardous work environment without the necessary Occupational Safety and Health Administration (OSHA) approved safety gear.

- Working without breaks. Unless you choose not to take a break, it is illegal in most states to not be given a 10 to 15 minute paid break every two hours. If you are a computer operator, you should definitely take a break to avoid repetitive motion injuries, such as carpal tunnel syndrome.

- Working in a capacity that is entirely different from the job description, as in the case mentioned earlier of the company that hired ten temps for office work and then sent them to a warehouse.

- Being asked to work on a project on your own time or to advance your own funds for business items, such as office supplies. It should also be noted that if you are asked to use your car for business activities, a mileage reimbursement fee should be agreed upon beforehand. This does not include your travel costs in getting to and from work.

- Being asked to sign as a witness to any legal document, contract, or court proceeding. As a temp, you should steer clear of signing any document that may make you a legally responsible party.

- Being asked to do something illegal, such as to forge someone else's signature on a document or even on a simple business letter.

When to Call It Quits

I have never had the occasion to quit an assignment suddenly. When I have quit, it's been because I've just gotten bored, or an assignment has gone on much longer than it was originally planned and I wanted out. Most of the clients that you are assigned to are known entities to the service who use temps on a regular basis and are careful of their public image. But, obviously, not every individual in every company is known to the service and there are some instances where just picking up and leaving are called for:

- If you are being sexually harassed (this topic is covered more fully in "Legal Issues" below).

- If you are otherwise threatened, either physically or verbally.
- If you know you are going to take the blame for an important project that's gone terribly wrong and it's not your fault.

Conflict Resolution

Most of your assignments will be enjoyable and should go off without a hitch. However, there will be instances where an unforeseen conflict will develop and tempers may flare. If you get yourself into a situation where you just can't see straight, always call your service and apprise them of the situation. In those situations, they will act on your behalf as your employer and as an honest broker.

Other times, you just need to vent and get an objective opinion. It's good to have a personnel coordinator who will listen. Usually, situations blow over if you just hang in there.

Getting Fired

It's a painful enough experience to get fired from a full-time job, but getting fired from a temporary job can be downright humiliating. Yet, it will happen. In most cases, it's just a simple matter of chemistry and you have to realize you can't please everyone all of the time. The service will not pay much attention to it and you'll soon get another assignment. Of course, if there are some legitimate complaints surrounding your dismissal or the same complaints occur again, then you will just not be called back by the service.

As I mentioned in a previous chapter, you may never know if you were fired. But one way to figure it out is if your assignment should abruptly end and no one can give you a plausible explanation for it. You may have been fired. In such cases it may be worth finding out exactly what happened because someone isn't telling you something, and that something may affect your reputation with the service.

I once had a two-week assignment in a major corporation, and right before quitting time on the first day my service called and said the assignment was over. I knew something was wrong but all the service could offer was that "things were just not working out."

This is what had happened: In the morning, my contact person at the company had instructed me to answer the phone on the second ring to give the full-timers a chance to answer it, on the reasoning that they would be in a better position to know how to handle the calls (sounded good to me). I was supposed to be a kind of back-up. But during the day, one of the full-time secretaries kept after me about answering the phone before the end of the first ring. I continued to answer the phone as I was instructed. I suspected what the problem was and, since the service didn't seem to know, I asked the contact person the nature of the complaint. Sure enough it was about the phones and it was from that secretary. I made sure that the contact person knew I was following the instructions and I informed the service of the same thing. I don't know what that secretary's problem was, but I do know that, as a temp, I need to keep my reputation intact with my service. That is my bread and butter. And if you doubted me before about how important that full-time support person is to your success, maybe now you won't.

If you are ever fired, or suspect you've been fired, first make sure that you have handled your responsibility correctly and then make sure your service has your side of the story, bolstered by the facts. Of course, if you see a potential conflict developing, it is best to try to straighten it out immediately, in a professional way, with the person who is the source of the conflict. I should have been more aware than I was and told this secretary (politely, of course) that I was doing as I was instructed and if there was a change, then let me know. But, of course, I didn't and got fired. The end result was that the service kept giving me assignments and there were no other complaints.

Legal Issues

There are a number of federal and state laws that protect all employees, including temporary workers, against discrimination, harassment, and unfair labor practices. These include:

The Equal Pay Act, which amended the Fair Labor Standards Act in 1963, prohibits the paying of wages based on sex by employers and unions. It provides that equal pay must be paid to workers for equal work if the jobs they perform require "equal skill, effort, and responsibility and are performed under similar working conditions."

Title VII of the Civil Rights Act of 1964 prohibits discrimination in the employment relationship. It applies to most employers engaged in interstate commerce with more than fifteen employees, labor organizations, and employment agencies. The Act applies to discrimination based on race, color, religion, sex, or national origin. Sex includes pregnancy, childbirth, or related medical conditions. The Act makes it illegal for employers to discriminate in hiring, discharging, compensation, or terms, conditions, and privileges of employment. Employment agencies may not discriminate when hiring or referring applicants. Labor organizations are also prohibited from basing membership or union classifications on race, color, religion, sex, or national origin.

The Age Discrimination in Employment Act (ADEA) prohibits employers from discriminating on the basis of age. An employee is protected from discrimination based on age if he or she is over 40.

Americans with Disabilities Act of 1990 and the Rehabilitation Act of 1973. The Americans with Disabilities Act was enacted to eliminate discrimination against those with handicaps. It prohibits discrimination based on a physical or mental handicap by employers engaging in interstate commerce and state governments. The Rehabilitation Act's purpose is to "promote and expand employment opportunities in the public and private sectors for handicapped individuals," through the elimination of discrimination and affirmative action programs. Employers covered by the Act include agencies of the federal government and employers receiving federal contracts over $2500 or federal financial assistance.

Complaints concerning discrimination issues should be brought to The Equal Employment Opportunity Commission (EEOC), which interprets and enforces the Equal Payment Act, Age Discrimination in Employment Act, Title VII, Americans with Disabilities Act, and sections of the Rehabilitation Act. The phone number can be found in the United States Government section of your local telephone directory. You can also bring your complaint to the Office of Civil Rights. In addition, many states and local municipalities have agencies that handle employment discrimination complaints.

Sexual Harassment: Sexual harassment occurs if your continued employment is contingent upon agreeing to an unwelcome sexual advance. It can also occur if a company allows a hostile work environment to exist; that is, a workplace where conduct of a sexual nature is permitted and interferes with a person's ability to perform her or his work. Sexual harassment can take many forms, from apparently innocent sexual remarks to unwanted physical contact to outright rape.

The fact that sexual harassment happens at all in the workplace is abominable. On the positive side, there is much more awareness of this issue than there was a decade ago. Many companies have taken positive steps to eliminate sexual harassment in the workplace by conducting workshops and putting in place internal procedures employees can follow if they feel they are a victim of sexual harassment. Still, sexual harassment is underreported. Nor are women its only victims.

Temporary workers are not necessarily immune from sexual harassment. The same laws that protect full-time workers also apply to temps. If you feel you are threatened sexually in any way, you should leave the premises immediately and report the incident to your service. You should make sure that the service follows up on your complaint with the client company. Because you are a temp, you may feel that just getting away from the situation and putting it behind you is enough. However, individuals who may sexually harass you are also likely to be harassing full-timers and possibly vendors. Perhaps they may be less likely to report these transgressions because they are afraid of losing a job or an account. It is your duty to make sure your complaints are heeded and pursued. If you feel the service is not doing enough, complaints concerning sexual harassment can and should also be brought to the EEOC. In addition, there are also state, city, and county agencies that handle such cases.

It is important to remember, however, that charges of alleged sexual harassment can have serious repercussions for the person accused, possibly resulting in the loss of a career as well as personal loss. Such charges should be well documented and supported before proceeding.

Discrimination by a Temporary Help Service: To say that temporary help companies or their employees are immune from violations of the law is to say that we live in a perfect world. Unfortunately, that is not the case. If you feel you are a victim of racial, gender, or religious discrimination or sexual harassment perpetrated by a temporary service, you have the same rights as an employee of any company and should immediately take the steps outlined above to protect those rights. Once again, all allegations should be well documented and fully supported before proceeding.

Injury: If you get injured while working a temporary job, you should be covered under your temporary help company's liability and workers' compensation insurance, which all companies should carry.

Overtime: Most states entitle you to overtime pay after you have worked 40 hours in a week. As a temporary employee, you are entitled to overtime pay from your service, even if the 40+ hours is spread among more than one client company.

Salary Disputes: You, of course, are entitled to the money you've earned. If you don't receive it, file a complaint with the state agency that handles wage issues. Filing a claim against the temp service in small claims or civil court, which-ever has jurisdiction in your area, may also be an appropri-ate action.

The Full-Time Job Offer: An offer of a full-time position is a legal issue, since just about all services have on the back of the time card a statement prohibiting you from accepting an offer of a full-time position or to otherwise work for a client except through that service for a specified period of time. The reason is that the service expects to be compen-sated for their loss of your income to them. They are entitled to some compensation since they are the ones who hired you and, in some cases, trained you or gave you the opportunity to upgrade your skills. If you are offered a full-time position, you should immediately contact your service. They will work out the details with the client. But even if you don't want the job, you should still contact your service. They may have another employee who might want the position.

CHAPTER 9

Temping Your Way to Full-Time Employment

Y ou've sent out hundreds of résumés, gone to dozens of interviews, and the best you've been able to get is a form letter thanking you for your interest. Don't get discouraged; try temp work. Don't underestimate the power of temping as a means of finding that full-time job, or just think of temping as a dead-end path with little or no future. Temporary help services do more than place fill-in secretaries or just-in-time labor. Today, many corporations view the temp as a possible full-time employee and many job seekers see temping as the way to a permanent position. The National Association of Temporary and Staffing Services (NATSS) seems to bear this out; it reports that nearly 40% of all temps are offered full-time jobs at the company to which they are assigned.

The reason is simple: As a temporary worker, you will have the inside position and the opportunity to demonstrate your talents and skills to a potential employer in actual, on-the-job situations. In addition, you

137

will be gaining the kind of experience in the skills that are most in demand in today's workplace. When that job opens up, who do you think the company will hire—someone who walks in off the street and fills out an application or someone who has been working in the company, who knows the company, and whom the company knows? The answer is obvious.

Getting A Better Paying Job, Too

There's another important reason why you should consider temping as a path to full-time employment: It has been shown that people who temp often get better, higher paying jobs because the pressure of earning a living while looking for work is reduced.

In a published report by the National Association of Temporary and Staffing Services, two studies conducted independently of one another found that people looking for full-time work ultimately obtained higher paying jobs after working as temps. According to the study conducted by Dr. Julie L. Hotchkiss, a professor at Georgia State University, an individual who takes a transitional job "may be better off in the long run because a transitional job will relieve enough financial pressure to give them the bargaining power to hold out for higher wages or a better job."

The studies also found that working as a temporary employee will not lessen your chances for full-time employment, and adds only five weeks to your job search.

Who Should Use Temping To Get Full-Time Work?

Probably everybody should consider temporary work as the bridge to full-time employment, but temping is the ideal way of getting a job if you are:

- In-between jobs
- Changing careers
- Returning to work after having been absent from the job market for a long period of time
- A college graduate
- New to an area
- Short on skills

Temping may become the only way of finding work in the future simply because everyone concerned—the prospective candidate and the company—has found that hiring a temp is cost-effective with little downside risk.

No Downside Risk to You

A few years ago, Forrest Gump, in the movie of the same name, said, "Life is like a box of chocolates; you never know what you're going to get." Life may be like that, but finding a full-time position through temping doesn't have to be. You can truly sample the merchandise and, if you don't like it, you can just throw it out and try another piece.

Temping gives you five distinct advantages over any other method of looking for full-time employment:

- The opportunity to sample and assess different industries and different companies in the same industry, so that you can see if you want to work for that industry or company.
- The opportunity to find out what benefits and other perks a company offers **before** going through the long and tedious process of applying for a job.
- The opportunity to get your foot in the door and to become a known and relied-upon asset at the company of your choice.
- The opportunity to become familiar and feel comfortable with a situation before going through a nerve-wracking interview process.

- The opportunity to get the private information of what job opportunities exist in the company before they become public knowledge (unlike insider trading, you won't get arrested for this information).

In addition, going this route enables you to:

- Get real-life experience that you can put on your résumé.
- Acquire new skills and brush up on old ones that will make you more marketable in many situations.
- Produce a better looking résumé, without the holes and gaps that can be so detrimental to any career.
- Develop and design a personal career path that suits your temperament.

There is also a psychological bonus in temping your way to full-time work—you are out in the marketplace doing something about your career. It will give you a better sense of yourself, while you are making money to pay the bills. Unlike Forrest's box of chocolates, finding full-time work through temping may be more like "Having your cake and eating it, too."

No Downside Risk to the Company

Of course, the Forrest Gump analogy holds true for the company as well. They have the opportunity to sample the merchandise—you—before they decide to hire you. Yvette Folk of Winston Staffing Services, Inc. calls this a "'try before you buy' situation."

Temporary help services, like a regular employment service, provide pre-tested, pre-screened employees, saving the company that step of the process. But there is one major difference. A temp service gives the company the advantage of seeing if the prospective employee is also a good fit for the company and the people with whom he or she will be working. And, often, no matter how well a person tests or appears on an interview, that person is still an unknown quantity until he or she is actually on the job and dealing with the people and normal stresses of the work environment. Using a temp service gives the company the added opportunity to get to know the candidate without making a commitment. The company can then take its time to evaluate the candidate in the actual work environment. When the company is ready to commit, the candidate has already proven his or her ability and the chances of getting stuck with a poor fit are reduced considerably. If the person doesn't appear to be a good fit, the company can just try another temp and all it has paid for are the hours the temp actually worked.

There are many cost factors involved in the hiring process, all of which can be significantly reduced by using the "try before you buy" method. Companies that choose to hire without using any intermediary have to pay for the cost of advertising, testing, and interviewing. In addition, there is also the time spent by human resources personnel in administering these tests and interviewing prospective candidates. All of this adds up when you consider the sad fact that qualified candidates are hard to come by. One major corporation, for example, found that fully 80 percent of the candidates it tests for support staff positions failed the basic tests and could not be hired. In an era where corporations need to concentrate on core business, having all of these extra human resources personnel to handle all of this testing and interviewing can be a tremendous waste of time, money, and energy.

Companies hire temps not only when they know they need a new permanent person, but also to test the viability of one. Let's say a company is growing. It knows that its employees are overworked but it doesn't know if there is a need for another full-time employee. In this situation, using a temp to determine whether there is enough work for another employee is cost-effective and efficient. It also has the advantage of taking some of the pressure off its already tired, full-time staff.

So successful is this arrangement that many companies now use temporary services exclusively to find full-time employees. And, quite frankly, what companies find successful should be important to you.

Why Would Companies Choose a Temporary Help Service Rather Than an Employment Service?

There was a time in the not too distant past when people seeking work went to an employment service, had an interview, gave the service a résumé and waited to get a call. Sometimes you waited for a long, long time. While you waited, perhaps you temped to pay the bills. Needless to say, temp services took notice of your needs and have moved into providing full-time work for their employees in a big way.

Temporary help services have a couple of distinct competitive advantages over a traditional employment service. They already have access to a large working pool of employees and they can structure their fees to make it more cost-effective for the corporation. Yvette Folk notes that traditional employment agencies charge their corporate clients a fee of one percent of your annual salary, which usually has to be paid in 30 days. "What happens if that person doesn't work out and you have to fire them three months later?" she says. "The company is back to square one."

Temp services don't work that way. If the company you are temping for wants to hire you, the service also charges a one percent fee. This so-called "liquidation fee" is a prorated fee, and usually turns out to be a lot less than the actual one percent charged by more traditional employment agencies. In addition, some of the very large temporary services charge no fee to the company at all. They consider it good will and rightly conclude that when that company needs another temp their service will be the one called to supply it. To say that this is a cost savings for a company looking for a permanent employee is to understate the case.

What Kind of Job Can I Get?

Okay, you're convinced that temping is the way to get a permanent job, but you're saying, "I don't really want a support staff job; I have the credentials and/or experience to work on a professional level." There are professional temp jobs available and we'll take a look at that more closely later, but no one looking for a permanent job should immediately dismiss working in a support staff position. The fact of the matter is, office-support work is much more plentiful and easier to come by and you never know where it will lead.

Finding full-time work through temping does not mean getting a job that is like your assignment; it means getting a job that you are qualified to do, in some cases without the experience that you would need if you applied through the regular channels. In a tight job market, it may be the only way of getting a job. That happened to me on my very first temping assignment.

I had one course to go to complete my college education and wanted to get a feel for what it was like to work for a corporation. I wasn't looking for a job, but I saw temping as a means to shop around and see what was available. I signed up with a service a friend recommended. A short time later, the service called with a three-week assignment as the secretary to an executive vice president of a large fundraising organization while the company sought a full-time replacement. I had no experience as a secretary, but my personnel coordinator assured me I could do the job and I took it.

As it happened, the assignment was in the marketing/communications department. Since I am a writer, I thought it would be nice to get the feel of corporate writing from the inside.

The job turned out to be a bore. I spent my days making paper clip designs on my desk, something the senior vice president of the department found hysterical. But, when I wasn't making happy faces with paper clips, I also read everything I could on what the company did and how the department worked. The paper-clip art notwithstanding, my initiative and desire to learn about the company was noted by other members of the department.

A few days after my assignment ended, I got a call from my service asking me to return to the company. The senior vice president's secretary had quit and I was requested back by the company to fill-in until a replacement was found. That desk was much busier and a lot more fun. I was working for three people, all of whom were writers. Along the way I mentioned that I was a writer, too. But, I still did not think about asking anyone for a job. That assignment lasted for a couple of months and when it was over, I was asked if I would return to help one of the other members of the department make phone calls to set up speaking engagements. That sounded like fun and I readily agreed.

During my stay on that assignment I was exposed to other parts of the department. In those three assignments I had pretty much come to learn a little about what everyone was doing from a lot of different angles. In that last assignment, the department's senior writer was fired. As I said, I wasn't looking for a job, but when one opened, I just felt that the position was meant for me. When I mentioned my desire to apply for the position, the members of the department gave me their full encouragement and support. So, I approached the person who headed up that particular section and who was someone I had worked for in my previous assignment and explained my intention. I should also note that the person who had quit had 14 years of corporate writing experience and I had none, zero, zilch. But I knew I could write and the company, at that point, knew me and liked me. They gave me a chance and I was asked to write a sample article. From that, the company asked me to write on a contract basis for three months. After that, the company hired me as their senior writer. During my four years there, I went from senior writer to director of editorial services. It was a great experience.

The point of this story is don't think the only jobs you can get are dead-end ones. There is no limit to what can happen. Sometimes you have to seek out a job and let people know that you are interested in full-time work. Sometimes a job just falls into your lap.

In my case, the company did not start out with the intention of hiring me and I did not start out with the intention of getting hired. Things just happened, and I was in the right spot at the right time. My experience is not unique; I have heard similar stories from many temps. This can also happen to you.

The Game Plan at the Temporary Help Service

Just like any endeavor you might pursue in life, having a plan of action is important to achieving success. Finding a full-time job through temping is no different. Fortunately, temping allows you to set your goals with a much broader brush stroke and gives you the opportunity to clarify your goals as you go from assignment to assignment, instead of having to know up-front exactly what it is you want to do. Still, you should have the basics in place to make your search more productive. These include:

- Writing a professional and up-to-date résumé that you can give to the personnel coordinator at the interview. (There are many excellent books on the market that provide information on how to write a résumé.)
- Selecting a service that has full-time opportunities or that deals specifically with temp-to-perm positions.
- Selecting a service that gets assignments in the field or industry you are most interested in finding work in.

Now that you've got the three main elements in place, it's time to talk to your personnel coordinator about your goals. People looking for work through a temporary service usually fall into one of four categories. Each category requires a slightly different approach and strategy. Let's take a look at how to approach each situation:

I Know What I Want: If you already know the type of work you want upon walking in, you are one step ahead of the game. Most people who are between jobs fall into this category. You already have a résumé that shows a work history with experience in your field. This will make your personnel coordinator's job easier and your search for work faster. Discuss your specific objectives with the personnel coordinator at the time of your sign-in interview. He or she will outline a strategy for getting you into the position and the industry you want, as well as determine the best way for you to proceed. If what you want to do is so well-defined that you know the company you want to work for, you should let your personnel coordinator know this as well, although you will probably not be able to find out if the service has that particular company as a client. Services will not usually tell you which clients they have, but you will be able to find out that information when you are sent out on assignments. Other temps who have worked for the service for a longer period of time also know who the service's clients are.

I Don't Know What I Want: There are certainly quite a few people who want to work full-time but really don't know what they want to do or where they want to do it. People who are interested in changing careers and recent college grads most often fall into this category. One of the pluses of temping is that it's not embarrassing to tell your personnel coordinator that you want to work full-time but don't really know what you want to do with the rest of your life. (Try telling this to a traditional employment service and see how far you'll get!) Temporary help services have a lot of experience in dealing with people just like you. Your personnel coordinator will be able to work with you and place you in a wide variety of industries and situations. Don't forget that 95 percent of companies in the U.S. use temporary workers. That means you'll be able to work in large corporate environments and small firms, in telecommunications or light industry, in advertising or finance. The list is literally endless. As you get more of a feel for what you want to do, you'll be able to go back to your personnel coordinator to narrow your search to those areas of most interest to you.

I Don't Have the Skills to Do What I Want: This is one of the areas where temping and temporary services really shine and is ideal for people re-entering the job market or those short on skills. Temping is a great place—perhaps *the* place—to gain hands-on experience and to acquire skills in up-to-date technologies that are marketable and in demand. Speak to the personnel coordinator about your goals and desires. You'll start out on assignments that just require common sense and responsibility. From there, take advantage of the free skills training and the cross-training opportunities. As you work your way up to more involved assignments, you'll be building your résumé, skills, and confidence all at the same time. Once you reach the point where you want to be, speak to your personnel coordinator again and tell him or her you're ready for that full-time position. If you've proven to be an asset to the service, you can be sure your personnel coordinator will begin placing you in assignments with full-time potential.

I Don't Have the Background: In today's job market, it is often the case that you can't get a job without having any experience. But how can you get experience if no one will hire you? It can be a very difficult Catch-22 situation, one that many college graduates face. Temping can be a solution here, as well. It certainly worked for me. Your personnel coordinator will be able to work with you to get you into the industries you want to work in. Even if you can't get the exact assignment you're looking for, temping will give you the opportunity to demonstrate your skills and make connections.

Assignment Strategies

Once you define what you need to get a full-time position from temporary work, you'll also want to put yourself in assignment situations that will lend themselves to achieving your goals.

Long-term assignments—those that are scheduled to go for a month or longer—are better if you are definite about where you want to work and are qualified to do so. They will give you the opportunity to prove yourself and make the connections necessary to get a job.

If you want to get a feel for what is happening in a particular industry or company, shorter assignments—those that can go for a day to a month—are for you. You'll be able to gain a broad perspective of your target industry in no time at all. Short-term assignments are also ideal for people who need hands-on experience in actual work situations. There's nothing like changing work environments every few days to see how things are done in different places and to gain experience rapidly.

Keep in mind, however, that no matter what your goals, at the beginning of your temp career, you want to be as flexible as possible. Your objective at the beginning is to form a good relationship with your service and to make money. Anything that you do for the service will work in your favor later.

The Game Plan at the Client Company

While your personnel coordinator can help you get into spots that have temp-to-perm possibilities and many services have official temp-to-perm programs (which we'll look at later in this chapter), much of getting a full-time position depends on your own ability. Once you're at a company where you'd like to work at full-time, it's really up to you to carry the ball and run with it. You obviously need to apply yourself to the assignment and to prove yourself, just like you would in all cases.

This means doing an excellent job, being punctual, conducting your-self at all times in a professional manner, and being a team player.

But if your objective is getting a full-time position, you'll need to do more than that. After all, what I just described is nothing more than what you would do in any situation and what the company expects you to do. You'll need to go that extra mile if you truly want a job and you'll need to communicate with people about your intentions. If you are on a long-term assignment, don't tell them right away; prove your-self first by working for a few weeks.

Show Interest: People are impressed when you not only know your job but have an idea of the bigger picture: what the department does and what the company does. It shows that you have a real interest in the company and that you are not just filling in. If you need to do research by going to a library, do it. Your bosses will be impressed by a temp who seems to know more than some of the full-time employees.

Tell Your Supervisor: Let your immediate supervisor know that you are interested in working for the company and in what area you are most interested. Getting a job does not necessarily mean going through a company's human resources department. Provide your supervisor with an up-to-date copy of your résumé, but only after you've been there for a few weeks and have had the opportunity to prove yourself and develop a rapport.

Speak to Other Department Heads: After you've spoken to your supervisor, you may want to explore the possibility of speaking to other department heads. However, make sure that you clear this with your on-the-job supervisor first.

Network: In addition to your immediate supervisor, speak to other full-time employees about your desire to work for the company. In many cases, they will know about possible openings even before human resources finds out about it.

Keep in mind, however, that you should use discretion in speaking with full-time employees, because you don't want them to get the idea you are after their job. Other temps can also be a good source of information, especially if they have been at the company longer than you. Once again, it is also important to use discretion when speaking with temps about positions in the company you are assigned to. Other temps may also be vying for a permanent position and may view you as competition if you speak too quickly. With both groups, it's best to lay the groundwork by finding out who you are speaking with before stating your intentions. And, since temps tend to get around, they may also be aware of openings in other companies and be willing to talk more openly about those positions.

Read the Company Newsletter: Many companies list positions internally first, before they go out on the market and advertise. If a company publishes a newsletter, that's a good place to check for possible openings. Mid-size companies may just post openings on a bulletin board. Being on the inside, you can take advantage of this information and find jobs that you could never discover otherwise.

Contact Human Resources: I put this down on the list even though I've never gotten a good job through human resources; in fact, I rarely ever get a response from human resources. Perhaps it's a good place for an outsider, maybe the only place, but you're an insider and there are better sources. Nevertheless, it is still a viable alternative to consider, especially if you are leaving the company. You can always submit your résumé, fill out an application, and ask them to keep your name on file for a possible future opening. But, once again, make sure you have the approval of your on-the-job supervisor before approaching the human resources department.

Get Recommendations: Getting recommendations from immediate supervisors can be invaluable in your search for a full-time job, not to mention your marketability as a temp. They can be used in the future, if you happen to see a job opening in the newspaper for that same company, or just as references when applying to jobs in other companies.

Follow Up: It's usually standard protocol to write a thank you letter after an interview. There is certainly nothing wrong with writing a thank you letter to your immediate supervisor after your assignment ends, reminding him of your desire to work full-time.

Go Through Channels: I've already mentioned a couple of times that you should get approval from your supervisor before going off in certain directions, but this procedure is worth a mention by itself. Corporations, especially large ones, are hierarchical and bureaucratic by nature and there's a correct way of doing something and an incorrect way. Going through channels is the correct way of doing things. If you become known as a person who goes off on your own to get what you want, your chances of getting hired will be diminished.

Don't Be a Pest: Another sure way of not getting a job at a company is by becoming a pest and constantly reminding your supervisor that you are looking for work. Having stated your intention and followed the procedures, if any, that your supervisor has recommended, you should go about your job. Of course, an occasional reminder is all right, but a weekly reminder is not recommended.

The "Temp-to-Perm" Way

Many services have combined the elements of a temporary help company with that of a traditional employment company in what is termed "temp-to-perm" positions. What this means is that, unlike an ordinary temp assignment which has a beginning and an end, temp-to-perm assignments are designed with the intention of making the position a permanent one. Of course, you need to tell your service that is what you are looking for and they will try to place you in these types of assignments. Naturally, you have to prove yourself to the company before they will hire you permanently. Thousands of people have gotten jobs in this way and the system has proven a successful one for all parties concerned: you, the service, and the company.

For you, it gives the opportunity of making money while still looking for full-time work, the chance to get to see a company from the inside, and hands-on experience to add to your résumé. Certainly a win situation for you.

For the company, they are getting a pre-screened, pre-tested employee who should be able to do the job. This saves them considerable money on training and recruiting fees, not to mention the loss of production from having an open slot. It further gives them a chance to find out more about you in actual on-the-job conditions before they make a commitment. Unlike using a traditional employment service, this option reduces a company's downside risk considerably because they are not paying you any benefits or making any commitment while you are temping. By the time they are ready to make that commitment, you have become a proven quantity and they know they want you onboard. Certainly a win situation for the company.

It is obvious that as far as you and the company are concerned, it is a good situation. But what's in it for your temporary service? After all, they are going to lose your money-making potential. Some services do charge the client a fee, but it's usually prorated and, in the scheme of things, not that important. So, what do they get? More temp business from the company. And that makes it a win for all concerned.

How It Works

When a client calls the service and tells it they are looking for a potential full-time employee, the service goes through its list of candidates, matching the skills and experience of the candidate with that requested by the client. Your personnel coordinator will also know if you have the personality and character to fit in with the corporate culture, assuring you a better chance of getting the job.

The candidate is then assigned to work for the company, as a temporary worker, for a trial period. This is the time when both you and the company can evaluate each other to see if there will be a good match. During the trial period, you remain an employee of the temporary service just like in any temporary assignment. The service still pays your wages, benefits, and any required insurance coverage, as well as deducts your taxes and social security. If and when you and the client agree to enter into a full-time employment relationship, your service to the temporary help company ends and you are placed on the client's payroll. You are not charged a fee by the service under this temp-to-perm situation. The service charges a fee to the company that has hired you.

Temp-to-perm placements do not release you from a company's probation period, normally three to six months. This period, which is a fairly standard practice, is meant to see if your motivation will endure. On the other hand, you may notice a difference in treatment before and after you are hired. Depending on the company, this treatment may not be better. If things don't work out, for whatever reason, and you have maintained a good relationship with your service, it will always take you back. Remember, you should never burn your bridges. In this era of lack of job security, you never know when you'll need that service again.

When You're Offered a Job

Whether you are looking for full-time work or not, there may come a time in your temp career when a supervisor will walk up to you and, out of the blue, ask if you would be interested in working for the company full-time. It's happened to me and it's happened to many temps in the course of their careers. Personally, I would not reject any offer out of hand, even if I was not looking for full-time work. It doesn't hurt to explore the offer more fully. Find out what the position pays; what the company benefits are (pension plan, insurance, health care); what you will get for vacations, personal days, sick days; and if there are bonuses, stock option plans, etc.

Obviously, one of the allures of a full-time position is getting a regular paycheck and having benefits. Weigh all the pros and cons carefully. Tell your supervisor that you would like a day or so to think it over.

Whatever your decision turns out to be, inform your temp service about the job opening. If you take the job, your service will have to work with the client in your transition from temp to permanent status and they will have to work out any financial arrangements between them. After all, your service has marketed you to its client companies, put you into the situation where you have been offered a full-time job, and may have helped upgrade your skills. It deserves to be compensated for your loss to them as a temporary worker.

If you do not take the position, your service may have someone else who is qualified and who may want the job. Remember, until you are actually hired, you are the employee of the service, and as such, you owe your allegiance to them. Besides, your service will appreciate the insider tip, which will only benefit you in the long run.

A Story of Perseverance

It would be nice if permanent jobs just fell into the laps of temp workers but, of course, that doesn't always happen. Temporary work can open the doors but the rest is up to you. Ask former temp worker Carl what it takes to get a full-time position and the first thing he'll tell you is "complete perseverance." Carl, who we met earlier, knows a lot about that topic because he worked at a company for two full years before he got the break he needed to get hired.

Carl was on his third assignment as a paralegal when he found the company he wanted to work for. "I just knew after a few days that this was the place for me. I liked the work and the people."

A month into his six-month assignment, Carl approached his supervisor and informed him that he wanted a full-time opportunity. Unfortunately, the company wasn't hiring at the time. "I kept at it and made sure my supervisor knew that I was still interested. Not every week because I didn't want him to get burned out on that much persistence but I mentioned it at least once every two months," he says.

Still nothing much came of his queries. At the end of his project, he was given another one because he had become known to other attorneys and was at this point a well-known entity at the company. The months passed and the projects kept coming. He was so trusted that he was often given work to take home. But he was still working as a temporary worker. "I admit, it did get frustrating at times. I could have called the service and asked them to place me in a position that had more chance of going full-time, but I wanted to work there and, as long as they were giving me work, I was willing to stay on."

Carl's big break came at an office party where he caught the attention of one of the senior partners who had never seen him before. "When I told him I was a temp and had been at the firm for two years, he was astonished." Two days later, Carl was hired.

"Had I not persevered and stuck to my goal, I would have never been at that place at that time. Now, I have a great job. It's wonderful."

Luck? Someone once said that we make our own luck. I think that's true and temping is a great place to get lucky. But, perhaps after reading about how wonderful temping is, you may be thinking you'd like to do it as a career. We'll take a look at that topic in the next chapter.

10

So, You've Decided to Make a Career of It

Now that you have a good idea of what temping is like, you may want to consider doing it as a career. Those that can be considered "career temps" comprise the second largest group of temps in the industry—about 38 percent. You may not start your life as a temp with the idea of doing it as a career, but along the way you may discover some very attractive features in temping that will help determine your decision. Perhaps it will come in that moment when you are offered a full-time position and you find yourself saying no. Perhaps it will come because, sadly, you search for a full-time job and find none. Perhaps it will come when that newborn looks into your eyes and you realize you want a lifestyle with more freedom and flexibility. Career temping is a great option for people who need some permanent flexibility in their lives, for retirees, or for people who are just fed up with the stresses and pressures of a full-time position.

There are as many reasons for choosing temping as a career as there are people who choose it. But for the most part, career temps have decided that being tied down to a permanent job and all the baggage that comes with it—corporate politics, dealing with a bureaucratic structure, living in fear of the dreaded pink slip—is not for them. Some may have decided that they want to spend more time with their families. Some may just want to feel independent.

The fact is, the sentiment that makes temping an acceptable career choice is echoed among full-time employees across the spectrum of the American corporation. Employees are looking for something other than work to satisfy their lives. In a 1993 Accountants on Call poll conducted nationally by the Gallup Organization, Inc., 66 percent of employees said they would prefer to work 10-hour days so they could have three days a week to spend with their families or pursue other interests. In another poll conducted by the Family and Work Institute of New York, 33 percent of employees said they would be willing to exchange salary and other benefits for the opportunity to be more personally involved with their children's upbringing.

While many employers now offer flex-time options to employees, they are often hesitant to take the company up on the offer for fear of having problems with advancement. Ah, if only these people knew the potential of working as a career temp. Would they choose that option? Would you? Your decision must really be based on what's important to you—and what isn't.

Profile of a Career Temp

Now, don't get me wrong, career temps are not people who will never take a full-time position. Nor are they lazy or unambitious or people who don't like to work. In fact, the opposite is true. Most of the career temps I've known are on the top of their service's call list, take on the most complicated and difficult assignments, work long hours and are always on call (what we call being available "24/7," or 24 hours a day, seven days a week). No, career temps certainly have no aversion to work. They may just want to work on a steady basis without the complication of making a long-term commitment or having to endure the same daily routine.

I would define a career temp as someone who:

- Has been temping for more than three years.
- Derives his or her income primarily or solely through temping.
- Would not presently consider any full-time position if it were offered.

The Advantages of Career Temping

If you have had a full-time job all of your life and have become accustomed to a steady paycheck, you might be wondering why someone would choose to make temping a career. Well, the fact is, you can do quite well at temping and still take advantage of life's pleasures. Here are some of the advantages:

Salary Without Stress: With career temping you can have a steady income without the stress and responsibility associated with having a full-time job. A temp job is not something you carry home after work; when the day is done, so is your responsibility. And most career temps, because they are highly skilled, experience very little involuntary downtime.

Freedom from Office Politics: Career temping provides you with the ability to remain free of the backstabbing and cutthroat environment found in many of today's workplaces. Can't take the politics? Just ask for reassignment.

A Feeling of Satisfaction: Since career temps are usually the most skilled and able, they are often called into the most difficult assignments or asked by the service to be the first temp for a new client. Career temps often feel a sense of satisfaction and accomplishment. Because they are so skilled, they may even be looked upon as mentors by other temps and employees where they are assigned.

A Balanced Lifestyle: Career temping offers you a greater ability to balance work and play and to pursue personal interests. As a career temp, you will be able to have control over the hours you want to work. You may choose, for example, to take on a long-term assignment with the relative financial security that it provides, or put in 80-hour weeks for a while, make a lot of money and then take some time off. The choice is yours.

A Multiple-Choice Lifestyle: As you have more control over the hours you want to work, you will also have more control over the environments you want to work in. Some temps want to work in specific industries, others for just one or two clients who give them steady work. Once again, the choice is yours.

Freedom from the Mundane: Every job can get boring, even a temp job. But temping gives you the possibility of an almost unlimited choice in the work you do. Tired of being a legal word processor? Then switch to the financial industry. Or get out of word processing altogether for awhile, don a rabbit suit and demonstrate a new product at the local mall. With temping there is always something new and challenging you can do. Temping never needs to get boring.

Opportunity to Meet New People: Temps meet new people everywhere they go. Career temps have it especially easy, since they are not competing with full-time employees or other temporary workers for often scarce full-time positions.

Learn New Skills: The doors to learning new skills are always open to the temporary worker. As a career temp, you can indulge yourself freely in the pursuit of knowledge. And, since career temps have established themselves with clients, oftentimes these steady temps will be offered the option to take in-house classes on new computer software programs.

The Disadvantages of Career Temping

There are many advantages to career temping, but there are also a number of distinct disadvantages. Since career temps are not looking to advance up the corporate ladder, that is not usually a concern. But finding a full-time job after temping very long-term may be more difficult. The reason is not because there is any stigma attached to temping. The reason is because long-term temps are seen by employers as more independent than the average corporate citizen and, quite frankly, many employers do not want to hire people who are seen as independent.

The major issue for a career temp, though, is the lack of healthcare benefits, life insurance programs, and pension plans. Career temps are certainly not alone when it comes to some of these issues—lack of healthcare benefits is a primary concern to millions of Americans.

While many services offer group healthcare plans, you still have to pay the full cost of coverage. You normally have to be employed by the service for 30 days before you are eligible to purchase the plan. Plans can be purchased on a long-term or short-term basis. A very few of the larger services will pay part of the premium. However, you have to work a certain number of hours to be eligible. Some services offer discount dental and prescription plans as well.

Providing for your comfortable retirement is another concern for career temps. While, as of this writing, the National Association of Temporary and Staffing Services has announced the endorsement of a 401(k) and retirement program, the plan is still too new to determine with any degree of accuracy how many temporary help companies will offer the plan and how many temps will find the plan to their liking. No doubt, there will be minimum requirements for eligibility as there are for group healthcare plans. Still, it is good to see that this most important issue is finally being addressed.

For the foreseeable future, the career temp may still find it necessary to obtain these benefits individually. That, unfortunately, is an expense that the career temp must take into account when calculating income. While it is an expense, it can be accomplished.

Career temps should consider joining a professional or social organization that offers group health benefits to its members if they don't wish to be dependent on meeting the minimum requirements for obtaining these benefits through a temporary service. I once joined a social organization that gave me access to group medical and dental insurance for a $40 per year membership fee. HMO plans are also worth looking into and are usually less expensive than buying individual health insurance. Likewise for pensions. Your best bet, if you plan on making temping a career, is to set up a tax-free savings plan by opening up an Individual Retirement Account (IRA) or a Keogh plan.

Sorting Priorities

Throughout the course of this book we've looked at temping as a means to get something else, such as getting a full-time job, gaining experience, getting a foot in the door, or paying bills until something else comes along. But the decision to be a career temp makes temping an end in itself. It is a good route to take for many, but it is not for everyone who temps. You can decide if career temping is right for you by sorting out what is and what is not important in your life.

- Do you need the assurance of a set amount of money every week?
- Are pensions and benefits on the top of your list?
- Do you need a mentor?
- Do you want to climb the corporate ladder?
- Do you need friends at work?

If you found most of the above important to you, then career temping may not be for you. On the other hand, if you find the following more important, then you may find great satisfaction in career temping:

- Do you have a hobby that brings in some money?
- Do you need more freedom and flexibility than you would get from a permanent job?
- Are you focused more on creative pursuits?
- Do you prefer diversity to sameness?
- Do you have an independent nature?
- Would you prefer a lifestyle that is not centered solely around a job?
- Are you entrepreneurial?
- Do you have access to health insurance from another source, for example, a spouse, membership in a guild or association, Medicare?

The Road to Career Temping

Once you've made your decision, there are definite steps you must follow to make a success of yourself. Being a success, at the very least, means paying the bills and still being able to do what you want to do with your life. With few exceptions, this involves work—sometimes as much work as you would put into any full-time job. The work that you'll need to do involves marketing yourself, making yourself indispensable, and keeping abreast of the latest developments in your field of expertise. None of this happens overnight.

Paul made $90,000 last year as a temporary legal word processor in New York City. That's even a good salary for an expensive city like New York. "Of course, I was working long hours on third shift," he says proudly.

Paul, who is 35, has a right to be proud because he's reached the pinnacle of the word processing temporary ladder. Paul started temping seriously five years ago when he decided that pursuing an acting career was never going to pay the bills. "It was a difficult thing to face up to the fact that I was not the next Tom Cruise, but I had been in acting for nine years and it was just time to move on. My problem was, what was I going to do for the rest of my life? Getting a job in a corporation was not at all appealing. I had been temping on and off throughout my acting career, so I thought I would continue doing that until I decided what to do next. I found I liked it so much that now I consider temping my career."

Paul explained his change of circumstances to his personnel coordinator who began to market him to his full potential. It took him another year to break into the big money but now he makes a consistent $50,000 per year, and there was that last year when he hit 90 grand.

Prerequisites of Career Temping

Despite a career temp's different needs, the one thing all career temps have in common is taking their careers very seriously. You must go for the highest paying assignments in the highest paying industries in your field. That means, for example, if you are in the office/clerical field, word processing would be the area you would want to work in. That also means signing up with those services that pay the best and have the best assignments. It means, in short, becoming an elite temp. These are some of the ways you can do it:

> **Know More Than the Basics:** While every temp should know more than just the minimal necessary to be successful, this is an absolute must for the career temp. It means keeping abreast of the latest technologies and trends.

> **Establish Yourself with the Service:** Career temps make money for their services on an extended basis and become the cornerstones in the services where they work. That means they can be relied upon to take on the tough assignments, even in the wee hours of the morning, if necessary.

> **Develop Your Client Base:** Career temps are known entities at a number of companies and have become indispensable

to them. They get called back again and again. Because they have proven to be such a value to these clients, they can also receive privileges, like taking a month off and being assured of a place back at the client company, that even full-timers don't enjoy.

Build Your Network of Temps: Networking with other temps is one of the best ways of finding out which services are busy and where the highest-paying work can be found. Career temps network with each other and help each other find work.

Making It a Business

If you like the idea of career temping, you may want to consider taking the next logical step in the process and try doing it on your own, without the benefit of using a service as an intermediary. This method is not for the faint of heart. Starting a business—any business—is risky and most people who start one usually do not succeed. It involves a lot of work and marketing, and requires providing a service that is in demand. While this approach may be more suitable to high-end temps, who are often already in business as consultants, I do know word processors who also get work independently. And while your business is growing, you can temp through a service to fill in the salary gaps. However, do not attempt to build your business by trying to take clients away from your service. It is not only illegal and unethical, it will quickly put an end to your business as well as your temp career.

There are two distinct advantages in making a business of it:

- Money. You can charge more per hour than you would make working through a temporary service, but because your overhead will be lower, less than what a service will charge a client.
- The potential to telecommute. With computers, modems, and fax machines, you may be able to find clients that will let you work from home—and that can be an added benefit.

However, there are also many disadvantages:

- The possible need—and legal expense—of creating a company or corporation.
- Dealing with Social Security deduction requirements and the filing of quarterly income tax statements with the Internal Revenue Service—not to mention all the paperwork that would be involved and/or the expense of an accountant.
- The possible need and expense of carrying insurance, such as workers compensation and disability insurance, as well as liability insurance.
- The need to carry receivables. When you work for a service, you get paid once a week. You don't have to worry about whether the service gets its money from the client company. When you are in business for yourself, you'll have to do your own billing and wait to get paid, 30, 60, sometimes 90 days.
- The need to have collection capability. And what if you don't get paid? Will you spend your time and money suing in small claims court or hire a collection service? Getting paid can be quite a hassle.

If you are doing something that millions of people can do, such as word processing, then you will also be competing with the temporary help services. While you may be able to beat them on price, companies will be hesitant to hire you. Services have the advantage of having hundreds of people at their disposal and can respond quickly. As an individual, you will not be able to offer that type of service. So, unless you have something unique to offer, going off on your own will be difficult. But, if you want to make a career of it, and are willing to put the time and effort into building a business, it may be something to think about.

High-End Temping

Doctor, lawyer, CEO? There's a whole new wave of temps out there who are not pounding keyboards or fitting widgets into gidgets. While office support jobs still make up 50 percent of the temporary industry and industrial jobs account for 25 percent, professional positions—such as doctors, lawyers, and CEOs—make up approximately 5 percent of the temporary workforce and are growing fast. That's right, temps no longer just process words, take dictation, or handle the switchboard; temps are now at the helm of large corporations, litigating cases, and treating patients. These high-end temps are making a name for themselves in the press and the workplace and, in the process, are putting the temping industry onto a whole new level. It has now become perfectly clear, thanks to this group, that temping is a very acceptable thing to do. In this chapter, we will take a look at this segment of the industry and at what drives an executive, an attorney, or a doctor to become a temp. We'll examine the pros and cons of temping on this level and, most importantly, how you may take advantage of this growing and exciting trend.

The Executive

Tom Rodenhauser, editor of the *Executive Recruiter News*, a publication that tracks the executive recruiter industry, calls it "the ultimate no-commitment job for the 90s."

While still comprising a very small segment of the temporary market, executive temping—specifically upper-level management, including the CEO, COO, and CFO job titles—is quickly taking its place as a respectable option to daily life in the upper echelons of the corporate strata. Demand for these high-enders has created a whole new industry virtually overnight. One indication of the meteoric rise in executive temping is the number of firms now in the business. There were just a handful of services in 1990 but in just five years that number has jumped to 300, which includes 19 services in other countries.

One of the reasons this is so, admittedly, is that the rarefied air of the corporate boardroom has, in many cases, become too thin to breathe. Many high-level executives saw their jobs downsized, rightsized, or re-engineered right out of existence during the cutback frenzy that seized corporate America at the beginning of this decade. Merger and acquisition activity, which had slowed for a while, began to pick up again by the mid-1990s and it can be assumed that the results will be the further loss of positions duplicated by these mergers and acquisitions. At the same time, an Internal Revenue Service crackdown on 1099 status left companies hesitant to contract independent consultants whose employment status may be questionable. The whole mix of reasons has created an ideal situation for the employment of interim executives.

As the trend catches on, corporations are finding the use of interim executives a valuable asset. In many cases, the interim exec is asked to come on board to handle a particularly difficult situation in a very specific area. "It is kind of a hired-gun type of mentality. The corporation asks you to come in, and it is short term; you're the person asked to do the turnaround," notes Rodenhauser. In addition, the highly experienced interim exec has found a valuable corporate niche in a mentoring capacity.

Who Does It

On any given day, there are more than 125,000 interim executives working in some of the country's largest corporations, oftentimes empowered to make decisions affecting thousands of people. This is certainly temping on an entirely different level. Who are these people?

Sally, with 15 years of executive experience, was the head of a human resources department for a financial institution that was on shaky ground. For some time the employees knew the company would go into bankruptcy. In exchange for a contractual financial agreement, Sally was asked to make sure things went smoothly until the end. However, when the end came, it came very suddenly. And when the company closed, Sally became one more experienced, highly qualified executive out of work. Yet she did not remain unemployed for long. Sally kept her skills sharp and kept her name in the industry by combining independent consulting and interim management work (a combination seen quite frequently in this sector of the temporary industry). "As it happened, I was able to manage both opportunities simultaneously. Financially speaking, it was a wonderful arrangement and gave me a lot more freedom to work my own hours. I found I liked it."

She liked it so much that, despite a number of job offers, Sally worked interim for four years. She finally accepted an attractive offer to run the human resources department of a company in the entertainment industry, a position that started as an interim one.

Like Sally, the people who are interim execs are not your young MBAs just out of graduate school. These people are highly skilled, highly experienced individuals who are used to making a minimum base salary of $75,000 per year. Many of them are in their mid-fifties. According to Sarah J. Marks, president of The Executive Source in New York City, a service that specializes in placing human resource management personnel, interim executives fall into two broad categories: those that are in-between jobs and those that are retired or are embarking on a second career.

Those in the first group have turned to temping because it's taking longer and longer to get jobs at the salary levels they are used to making. An interim exec who is in-between jobs is able to keep his or her skills fresh and use them as a way of staying in the market. Of course, there's always the potential for an interim job to turn into a full-time one.

The other group is a rather interesting one because it is made up of people who really don't want to work as an employee, don't need to work, and certainly don't want to work a full year. These include people who are pursuing personal goals, independent consultants in-between projects, early retirees, and downsized executives who have landed safely with the benefit of a golden parachute. In a very real sense, these high-enders can be considered career temps who have discovered a lifestyle unburdened by long-term commitments and obligations. This group makes up a very large proportion of the interim executive field. Marks notes that almost 50 percent of the interim execs placed on assignment through her service fall into this category.

No matter what category you fall into, the successful interim appears to be an individual with a broad-based general knowledge of his or her field, and a hands-on type who is capable of hitting the ground running. "It's not a job for shrinking violets," says Sally.

The Pluses and Minuses

If you find yourself wanting or needing to join the ranks of this small elite group of professionals, you'll discover there are many benefits to this workstyle. These include:

- The ability to generate income between consulting or independent contracting projects.

- The ability to generate income while searching for a permanent position.

- The opportunity to maintain a clean and viable résumé, without holes or gaps, during a job search.

- The opportunity to network, make valuable contacts, and gain future references—even if a particular assignment doesn't have a chance of going permanent.

- The chance to regain some self-respect, which sure beats sitting in a cubicle in a company-financed outplacement center making calls to nowhere. There is no stigma attached to being an interim; unemployed executives, however, may have to deal with negative perceptions.

- The opportunity to gain experience, usually in high-pressure situations.

- A great way to hone interview skills.

- The possibility that the position may go permanent or that you will have the inside track on a future position.

- The opportunity to travel, nationally and internationally, especially since the end of the Cold War and the signing of NAFTA. There are many opportunities opening up in former Communist-bloc countries since there are very few executives in these countries who have free-market economy experience. Opportunities also exist in U.S.-based export companies. Assignments abroad can last for up to three years, as opposed to the six-month assignment length in the U.S.

- The ability to have more control over your schedule and to create a personal lifestyle of your choosing. Positions may be for only a few days a week for a specified period, or you may be able to do a project from the comfort of your own home.

As you can see, there are many pluses to becoming an interim executive. But, there are also a number of minuses. These include:

- A lack of benefits, such as medical and hospitalization plans.

- Difficult to temp and look for full-time employment at the same time.
- Positions are highly specialized.
- Difficult to estimate income. Like every temp job, of course, if you don't work, you don't get paid. Executive temps also have to deal with wildly fluctuating salary ranges. One assignment may be for $900 per day; the next, $500 per day.
- Not much chance of seeing your temp position go to permanent status.
- The possible stigma of being an interim executive long-term if you are looking for a full-time position. It is an unfortunate fact in our society that anyone who has been out of work too long may become unemployable. This is certainly true of the executive. Currently, there is no stigma attached to doing this short-term, and it is expected that any negativity attached to doing interim executive work long-term will largely become a thing of the past. In fact, with the project-oriented focus of most corporations, the abilities of an interim exec may become the most prized.

One of the major differences between this type of temping and all other types is in the chance of seeing your temp job go permanent. Companies rarely bring in an interim exec as a potential candidate when a permanent slot opens up. Only about 15 percent of interim executives are asked if they want to stay onboard in a permanent capacity. This compares unfavorably to the temporary industry average of 38 percent. Whether this situation will change or not remains to be seen. But even if it does, it will only do so for the highly experienced and seasoned executive. Interim executive temping will most likely never be the place for recent MBAs or those with limited corporate experience.

As already noted, the interim exec is usually a person over the age of 55 with many years of managerial experience. Companies seek out these talented executives, who are often overqualified for the tasks they perform, for highly specific projects. Their ability to come into an unknown situation and to come up to speed quickly are the qualities prized by the client.

Hot Industries and Functions

Since the interim executive field is still so new and expanding rapidly, it's difficult to pin down exactly which industries and job categories offer the most significant opportunities for those entering the field. On the other hand, if you, as an executive, want to try temping, it's important for you to know if your qualifications can be matched successfully.

Kennedy Publications, which publishes a directory of executive placement firms (listed on this page), tracks the placement of interim executives by industry and function among firms that deal with executive placement. In an estimate published in its 1995 edition, the top five industries were Manufacturing, High Tech/Electronics, Finance, Communications, and Services. The top five functions were Finance & Accounting, Information Technology, Human Resource Management, Sales & Marketing, and General Management.

Selecting a Service

On a variation of the traditional executive placement firm that calls an executive from one company with a fantastic job offer at another company, you may not have to find a service—it will find you. But the call that you get will not be for another job. Instead the call will come because it's become general knowledge that your company is downsizing and the placement counselor on the other end of the firm wants to know if you would like to become an interim executive. It may not be the call that you would want to get, but it does indicate the strength of this particular market sector.

If you don't get such a call, then other than asking a colleague or responding to an ad in the newspaper, the most comprehensive list of executive search firms can be found in:

The Directory of Executive Temporary Placement Firms, published by Kennedy Publications in Fitzwilliam, New

173

Hampshire, lists services by function and industry and provides a brief sketch of each service.
1-800-531-0007
Price: $24.95.

Or you can send a stamped, self-addressed envelope with a request for the list of professional temporary help services to:

The National Association of Temporary and Staffing Services (See address on page 66.)

Once you've found a service that seems suitable to you, you will want to make sure that the service handles your line of work. There are numerous services that cover a broad range of job titles, but many specialize in specific areas. Some handle executive search/recruiting and outplacement as well as executive temporary placement. Depending on your needs, you should target only those services that meet your criteria. You should also find out how the service is categorizing you for tax purposes. Will they treat you as an employee, or as an independent contractor? Most services treat you as an independent contractor, which means you will be required to pay all of your required withholding amounts yourself. Since so many people in this industry are independent consultants, who already own their own business and are, therefore, legally set up to handle the paperwork, this may not be a consideration for you. However, if you prefer an employer/employee relationship, you will want to make sure the service can accommodate your needs before you make a commitment.

It is important when creating your résumé to include the specifics of all completed projects, since most of the work available to interim executives is project-oriented. If you've done interim work before, be sure to note especially those assignments that you took on with little or no advance notice and those that were accomplished under very tight deadline pressure, since that's the type of work you will most likely be called on to do. The ideal interim candidate is a person capable of coming up to speed very quickly on a project and who doesn't need to ask many questions before jumping in.

Marketing Yourself

Once you've sent a cover letter and résumé to the service, you probably won't get an interview until there is an opening for your specific qualifications or there at least appears to be something coming up on the horizon. However, Sarah Marks' firm, The Executive Source, does make a special effort to see all applicants who come to them via personal recommendation. Her firm also sends out a thank-you letter with an enclosed four-page applicant data summary sheet, which allows the candidate to give more detail than can ordinarily fit onto a résumé.

Services usually enter the information they receive from you into a database which then matches the client's requirements with possible candidates. Once you've been selected, you can expect to get an interview from the service (if you haven't had one from a previous assignment), as well as at least one interview at the client company (but more likely two or three interviews). Depending on the level of executive you are, board approval may also be necessary. Despite the necessary red tape in securing an interim exec position, the process is much faster than it would be for the same job if it were full-time. Marks notes that it usually takes a week from the time a call is placed by a client company to the decision, whereas it would take many months for that same individual to get a full-time job—even if the interim job and the full-time job have the exact job description. This, of course, means that you can be in a decision-making capacity and making a good income in rather short order.

Getting that first assignment, however, may require just a little bit of self-marketing. For example, Marks recommends that anyone applying to her service should call about a week after sending the summary data sheet just to check in. She also notes that, if you haven't heard from the service in a while, to send a letter every few months, detailing your activities. "When we get a letter from someone, it gives us another chance to open up the file and to think about that person. This may initiate a phone call which will lead to an assignment," she explains.

In general, it is acceptable policy to check in with the service from time to time to let them know what is going on with you. However, it is equally important to get to know the name of a principal or a recruiter at the service that you can contact. As in the temporary industry, in general, despite talk of high-tech computer matching programs, this is a people business and when you don't stay in touch, you won't be in touch.

The Assignment

Interim executives are often called in to do very specific jobs, sometimes unpleasant ones, such as reorganizing a department or company, bringing a company back from the brink of bankruptcy, or re-enforcing company policies that have become lax. Perhaps that's why interim executives are referred to often as "Business Commando."

Since interim execs often have far-reaching authority and decision-making power, it is important to make sure that everything be spelled out clearly to avoid possible conflict down the line. For example, on one of her assignments, Sally wrote a letter of agreement for the company director that clearly stated her authority. Then she sent a memo under the director's name to the company employees, informing them of her duties and authority. Sally recommends that interim execs should make it clear from the beginning what their job description entails and to have it in writing.

Getting Full-Time Work

Despite the low rate—about 15 percent—of interim execs who get offered full-time positions through temping, those figures should not discourage anyone from the hope of finding a full-time position. As a former executive, you have already "beaten the odds" by climbing the corporate ladder successfully. You have also developed plenty of skills along the way. Although your ego and your pocketbook may have been damaged due to a recent cutback or similar situation, the ability to turn a bad situation into a good one is strictly within your control.

During a six-month assignment, a lot can happen. Patience and the ability to create opportunities are important traits to develop. Marks has heard of many stories where interims have literally "pitched themselves into a full-time job." They have made presentations on very senior levels demonstrating the need for a full-time position and the reasons why they were the ones to do the job. And we're talking jobs at the top of the corporate hierarchy. So, rather than looking at the statistics, just go for it!

Attorney at Law

Less than a decade ago, the idea that attorneys would even consider becoming temporary workers—let alone that it would be a popular and acceptable option—would probably have been scoffed at by those in the legal profession. But a lot has changed. Most notably, the boom cycle of the late 80s has ended and the legal profession was especially hard hit. Many major law firms reduced their staffs dramatically or stopped offering partnerships to associates. Some just simply disappeared. All this with about 40,000 students graduating from law schools each year. There are just not enough jobs to go around anymore. By the early 1990s, legal temping on a grand scale had arrived. What a difference a few years can make!

"The recession put many highly qualified professionals into the job market, and in that job market, temping took on a new appeal as an alternative to job searching that started at square one," says Derek Kipp, communications director of Special Counsel International located in New York City, a temporary service specializing in placing attorneys.

177

What started as an effect to an economic cause has now definitely turned into a trend with no signs of diminishing. In fact, with a growth rate of 35 percent per year, it seems like the era of the temporary attorney is here to stay. "The legal niche will grow at an especially fast rate, as it is just now gaining national recognition, attention, and acceptance. I believe the legal temporary concept is now a regular component of law firm management," states Bryce Arrowood, president of LawCorps® Legal Staffing Services in Washington, D.C., another service that handles temporary attorneys, as well as paralegals.

It does seem that hiring temp attorneys is ideally suited to the legal industry. This is because the legal community experiences wildly fluctuating cycles that are largely dependent on business cycles and client needs. Arthur worked as a full-time lawyer for 10 years before deciding to become a temporary attorney. He has seen the legal industry change dramatically over the last few years. His view of why attorneys temp comes from the individual perspective, rather than the firm's perspective. He sees an industry in which "the opportunities are different. The stereotypic idea of the partnership track is just not as widely available as it once was. The attorneys who temp said, 'Why should I stay at a firm that's not going to reward me in the way that I want, when there's this other option where I can work in a variety of ways and make good money with time off?'"

The same can be said of the legal departments in large corporations. While they may need a minimum number of attorneys on staff at all times, major corporate maneuvers may require additional attorneys for set periods of time to handle the overflow legal work.

The Contract Lawyer Profile

Just like the temporary field in general, attorneys who go into contract lawyering span the full spectrum of categories. Many do it because they can't find a job with a law firm, so they temp to pay bills and student loans. Others do it because they want to explore a new practice area and view temping as a means of gaining experience in a field they are not familiar with. Legal temping is also ideal for those with a law degree who are studying for or waiting for the results of their State Bar exam. Then there are those who are checking out the legal environment. Likewise, it is a good place to begin for a recent law school graduate just entering the legal market. And it is certainly the ideal choice for those who want to remain professionally active while they raise a family or pursue personal interests.

Surprisingly, many attorneys are temping because they choose to temp. They find contract lawyering to have many pluses. These include the freedom and flexibility to pursue interests other than lawyering, while still remaining professionally active. Some attorneys also use contract lawyering as a way of earning income while building up their own solo practices. "More and more professionals are choosing to temp," says Kipp of Special Counsel. "And that in itself is something we consider remarkable, considering that not long ago, temping was stigmatized as a resource for the desperate."

A quick scan of the classified section of any major newspaper would prove that temping for attorneys is certainly not a resource for the desperate. Many temporary help companies and recruiting firms are seeking only attorneys from top law schools who have made Law Review or attorneys with extensive large law firm experience.

Garnering respect from companies and peers is no problem for these top attorneys. "The attorneys we place are thoroughly qualified, often coming from law firm or corporate environments comparable to the setting of their assignment, with credentials comparable to the lawyers they'll be working alongside," Kipp said. "Any stigma related to temping is, in the temporary attorney field, a thing of the past."

Finding a Legal Temporary Service

At present, there are approximately 30 legal temporary services in the U.S. However, services specializing in legal-only staffing are springing up all over, now that legal temping has gained wide acceptance and popularity. In addition, general staffing services are adding legal departments. As a professional, you want to make sure that you pick a service that's right for you and that has gained respect in the legal community. Since services may tend to specialize in specific practice areas, it is equally important to pinpoint those services that have work in the area of practice that interests you. Here are some suggestions on how to begin your search:

- Ask colleagues and friends. They may have heard of a service that deals with legal temping or their firm may have used a legal temporary service.
- Read the local and national legal periodicals.
- Check the Sunday classifieds in the major newspapers.

Once you have an idea of which services handle which specialties, application is made strictly through the mail. Most services do not even allow phone calls. A detailed and professional cover letter is, therefore, an absolute necessity, since it will be the only contact you will have with the service until you are called. The cover letter should be addressed to the right person at the service. Form letters should be avoided at all costs. Along with the cover letter, you should also submit your curricula vitae, one page if possible, including work you've done on short notice.

After you have submitted your cover letter and résumé, there is little else you can do except wait. Most services will not even call you in until there is a specific assignment available that matches your criteria. When it comes to legal temping, patience is definitely a virtue, but one that will pay off in the long run.

When something that appears to match your qualifications surfaces, you will be asked to come in for an interview and to go through what is usually an extensive and in-depth registration process. Of course, once you've had an assignment through the service, you will not need to go through the process each time a possible assignment comes in.

A list of interested candidates that matches the client's criteria will be submitted to the company. You will then be interviewed by the client company who ultimately makes the final decision. Your conduct and professionalism at both the service and client company interviews is extremely important to successfully landing the assignment. In addition, the client will want to ascertain if you have the knowledge needed to do the job, since, in most cases, you will have a very short learning curve. You most likely will be tested by the client company or firm as part of the interview process. Once you get an assignment, you can expect it to last an average of six months.

Since attorneys handle confidential and privileged information, one of the concerns about hiring a legal temp has been the ability to check for possible conflicts of interest and ethical considerations. For a time, bar associations were not in favor of legal temping because of this. These issues turned out to be needless worries. Contract attorneys are professionals and know they are bound by the same code of ethics regarding confidentiality and conflicts of interest as any attorney. Eventually, the bar associations had to rule that temp attorneys did not violate any codes simply by temping and that, too, helped open the flood gates.

Getting Full-Time Work Through Contract Lawyering

The "hit rate" for those looking for full-time work through contract lawyering is not exceptional, approximately 15 - 25 percent. If you are desperate for a job, this may tempt you to market yourself heavily in the hope of pushing yourself into a full-time slot. Arrowood, however, recommends against blatant lobbying for permanent employment. "Law firms are extremely sensitive to this tactic," he states.

Instead, he recommends impressing a firm through your actions. Eagerness, motivation, a good attitude, and hard work pay off in the end. Even if you don't get a job at a particular firm, remember there are other firms your service can place you with.

In the end, proving yourself and becoming indispensable to your service is just as important as doing a good job on assignment. When you accept all kinds of assignments on short notice and show your flexibility, your service is more likely to work harder for you. Arthur, who now would accept a full-time job if it were offered to him, has developed such a relationship. "If my service could hire me, they would do it in a second," he says. "They have treated me well and I have treated them well. They respect me and have told me they consider it a goal of the organization to place me. I feel positive and optimistic. And I've developed a great relationship with them."

As with so much in the industry, a lot depends on your ability to get the people in your service behind you. Once you do, you can beat the odds—even in the competitive field of contract lawyering.

Is There a Doctor in the House?

It's called *locum tenens*—Latin for "one holding place"—and unlike the other two professional temping categories that have been looked at in this chapter, the idea of locum tenens has been around for quite a long time. Locum tenens began about 25 years ago as a means of providing needed physician services to medically underserved areas, such as in rural health clinics. In those early days, the type of physician that filled such a role was not usually well regarded. As the idea caught on, however, locum tenens physicians were increasingly used to replace vacationing physicians and doctors who were pursuing continuing education. With the vast changes that have occurred in the medical field and medical care, the locum tenens option has gained wider acceptance and, with that, newfound respect. Many desirable positions are now filled by locum tenens physicians nationwide, in the big city hospitals as well as in the rural townships.

Who Does It

Today's approximately 15,000 locum tenens are mostly young physicians just out of residency. For the most part, they are men and women who want to experience different practice settings in different areas of the country before making a career decision. Doing locum tenens work gives these people the opportunity to observe firsthand a practice setting before having to commit to it. With so many choices available, becoming a locum tenens may be one of the best ways a young physician can really narrow down his or her options.

Jamie, a board certified family practitioner now working full time at a large HMO in Albuquerque, New Mexico, found locum tenens to be the ideal solution to his decision-making process. As a resident in Virginia, Jamie thought he knew what he wanted to do for the rest of his life. He had planned to practice medicine as a civilian contractor with the U.S. military in Germany. He did not anticipate the end of the cold war and the resultant closings of so many military bases. By the time he was finishing his residency, job opportunities for doctors with the military in Europe were practically nonexistent. With the end of that dream, Jamie found a new dream when a friend pointed out an ad for a service specializing in locum tenens. "The idea of doing locums struck me as exciting, since, at that point, I wasn't ready to settle into a practice right away. I saw it as a good way to see the country and decide where I wanted to work and where I wanted to live."

Jamie worked locums for three years before settling in the Southwest, during which time he had the opportunity to work and experience many different practice settings, including private practice, small groups, and big HMOs. He even did a stint on an Indian reservation, an assignment he liked so much, he went back a second time.

If you are a young physician, fresh out of residency, locums is an excellent way to help you decide what you'd like to do, make a good income, and see the country, all expenses paid. In addition to gaining experience and narrowing down your goals, locums is ideal for:

- Physicians who are going into a fellowship and who need to fill up the period between the end of their residency and the beginning of their fellowship. Locums can be an ideal way to pay off some medical school debts and gain some experience while you're waiting for your fellowship to begin.

- Physicians who can't begin their preferred practice choice because they've finished their residencies or fellowships at an off-time.

- Doctors who are in mid-career and want a change of practice setting or scenery.

- Semi-retired doctors who want to remain professionally active.

Hassle-Free Medicine

One of the chief benefits of doing locums work is its ability to provide you with a good income while incurring very little out-of-pocket expenses. Most locums can expect to enjoy salaries upwards of $100,000 per year for a 40-hour week, 40 weeks per year. The locum tenens service will also pay for your lodging accommodations and all transportation, including airfare and a rental car while on assignment. So, except for entertainment expenses, there is very little that you need to pay for, and saving on lodging costs can add a significant amount to your income. And these extra benefits are not considered taxable income.

In addition, the locum service will also pay for your malpractice insurance, as well as handle state licensing and hospital privileges. Your only responsibility is to provide identification and educational and professional credentials and, as Jamie notes, to "just sign on the dotted line." The service handles all the details. You should, however, read your malpractice policy carefully to make sure it contains sufficient coverage and will still protect you from claims filed after you've left locum tenens work.

Because licensing is a state procedure, you should also keep in mind that some assignment planning may be necessary. If your preference is to work in a state that takes a notoriously long time to issue a license, you may not be able to get an assignment in those states as soon as you sign up. You can take an assignment in another state while your license is being approved in the state of your choice.

There are a number of other advantages to choosing locums work besides the ability to practice medicine without some of the burdens regular physicians face. These include:

Variety: A locum tenens physician gets the opportunity to sample a wide variety of practice settings without having to make a commitment to any particular practice. Like Jamie, it will help you make an educated decision when the time is right.

Travel: Another big attraction of locum tenens work is travel—all expenses paid. Jamie traveled all over the country in his three years as a locums. He spent time in Colorado, Utah, New Mexico, California, Arizona, Georgia, North Carolina, and Hawaii. But there are also assignments that travel with you. How about taking an assignment on a cruise ship, for example? How about a cruise ship that's making a port of call in Hawaii? And they pay you for this stuff, too!

Experience: Locums gain a wide range of medical experience across all different types of practice settings—experience that may be crucial to your ability to negotiate a good full-time position down the line. In addition, you'll see firsthand how different offices are run administratively, things you just don't learn in medical school and residency.

Flexibility and Control: And finally, as in all temporary assignments, locum tenens will offer you maximum control over your schedule, letting you pursue lifestyle choices.

The Disadvantages

Yes, there are some minuses to being a locum tenens physician, most of which have to do with travel:

Travel: While seeing the country at someone else's expense may be exciting, constantly being on the road has some distinct disadvantages. Unlike other forms of temping, traveling for a locum tenens is not a voluntary option. And while it is possible to land a long-term assignment, the vast majority last between 4-6 weeks. If you don't like to travel, being a locum is not for you.

Travel means you can expect to be doing a lot of packing and unpacking and trying to find your way around unfamiliar settings. This can lead to loneliness and a sense of isolation. Female physicians, particularly, may not feel comfortable about navigating unfamiliar cities and locales alone. One antidote to this feeling of aloneness would be to have a laptop computer and an e-mail service. This will allow you to stay in touch with family and friends. And it's a lot less expensive than the telephone.

Relationship Stress: If you have a spouse and children, being constantly away can put an inordinate amount of stress on family relationships. This is why locum tenens is ideally suited for young, unattached physicians or elderly physicians who can bring their spouses with them. Physicians with school-aged children, for example, may find this type of lifestyle extremely difficult.

Patient Unfamiliarity: While you have probably learned to maintain a professional detachment from your patients, it may be a particularly frustrating experience to have to leave patients in the middle of treatment. There may also be difficulties in picking up where another physician left off, especially if the previous physician did something wrong. This type of transitional care can lend itself to professional liability claims. Although your malpractice insurance is covered by your service, no one wants to get involved in a legal hassle with the resultant record in the National Practitioner Data Bank. It is important, therefore, for every locum tenens physician to keep extremely accurate and precise records to cover him- or herself.

No Benefits: Except for malpractice insurance, there are no other benefits, such as company-paid health insurance, paid vacation or sick days, etc. Services do offer health and dental plans, but you would have to pay the premiums.

No Career Track: Also consistent with other forms of temping, one of the drawbacks to locums work is the inability to achieve advancement or to climb the organizational ladder.

Point of Diminishing Returns: In addition to having no career track, doing this type of temping can have a negative impact on your career if pursued long-term, especially if you are a young physician looking for a job. While you should encounter no problem with peer respect as a locum, you may be looked at somewhat askance if you remained a locum for as long as five years. For semi-retired physicians, however, length of service as a locum would have no stigma attached to it.

If you think the advantages outweigh the disadvantages, then locum tenens is something you should definitely consider.

Finding a Locum Tenens Service

There are about 30 services in the United States that specialize in locum tenens positions, of which CompHealth/Kron in Salt Lake City,

Utah, is, by far, the largest. When looking for a position, you may want to:

- Ask a colleague.
- Respond to an advertisement in a professional journal.
- Go off on your own with help from the American Medical Association. Although most positions are found through services, some doctors choose to contract out on their own. The American Medical Association has its own locum tenens service, and maintains a list of locum tenens opportunities in its Opportunity Placement Register. For more information about these positions or for guidelines on being an independent, call the AMA's Physicians Career Resource at 800-955-3565.

Since there are so few services that specialize in this field, you may wish to telephone all of them to get an idea of what is being offered. Once you find one that you like, send a letter and curricula vitae to the individual you've spoken to. Make sure you do not send a form letter. There is a large demand for locum physicians, so you shouldn't have long to wait for a reply. In addition to speaking to them over the phone, you will also be interviewed in person. If you are not in the same city as the service, it will fly you out at company expense.

Contract Negotiations

As a locum tenens physician, you will be considered an independent contractor with a contract between you and the service. Different services have different contract policies, but some of the more common clauses include agreement on the number of weeks per year you would be under obligation to work, and assignment length. You may also be offered a contract that guarantees you a salary even if the service is unable to find you work, or one that gives you complete control over working arrangements.

Remember, a contract is essentially an agreement reached between two parties and, while there may be certain standard clauses among the services, you will be able to negotiate a contract that best serves your needs. Contract negotiations can range from the major, such as assignment particulars, to the seemingly minor. Jamie, for example, wanted his 10-speed bicycle shipped at company expense to all of his assignments. His bicycle was important to him and he made sure to have it included in his contract. So, if you have any needs or requirements, now is the time to negotiate and have them written into the contract. Of course, you should also read and make sure you understand the contract before you sign it.

Finding Full-Time Work as a Locum

There are no formal temporary to full-time procedures in the locum tenens field. You are, therefore, strictly on your own when it comes to obtaining a job. However, since most assignments exist because a practice is short a doctor, there are many opportunities to obtain full-time employment wherever you go. Jamie, for example, was offered a job on practically every assignment. In his three years as a locum physician, he had approximately 30 assignments, so that translates into a lot of job offers.

Obviously, the surest way of finding work through practicing as a locum tenens is to do a great job on assignments and, like all other temporary positions, to be flexible. Jamie discovered that working with his service and accepting all types of assignments provided opportunities he had never expected. Looking back upon a successful locum tenens career he says, "You have to be able to look for opportunities in the ways in which they come to you. Just take things as they come, because great things will come."

You're on
Your Way

Now that you've gotten the inside scoop on temping, you should use this knowledge to make your experience a successful one. If you're new to temping, you'll be able to get going more quickly and intelligently. If you've been doing it for a while, you'll be able to get better paying assignments.

Keep in mind that temping is a lot like building your own business: The more you put into it, the more you'll get out of it. Develop those solid relationships with your personnel coordinator, network and communicate, build a base of client companies that keep calling you back, and most important of all, be flexible. Just about everyone in this book, from the insiders in the temping industry to the temps getting the best assignments, have said that flexibility is the key ingredient to this business. Keep in mind this formula:

Flexibility = Success

It will set you on your way to getting the opportunities that temporary work offers: open doors to full-time positions at a higher rate of pay, more control over your schedule and life, the chance to learn new things and meet new people, and a high rate of job satisfaction. That last item, I was happy to find out in the course of writing this book, is something that seems to be a resounding refrain among quite a few temps. Quite honestly, I did not expect to discover it among the high-enders in this field. But it was good to know that even an executive, a doctor, or a lawyer can find such a high degree of job satisfaction working a temporary job, since so many of us will find ourselves temping in the next decade. Now we have proof from all sectors that one can find happiness in temping. That, of course, is in your control.

This book has given you the tools you need to be successful. What I hope it has also done is given you the correct attitude towards it. A positive attitude, as you've gathered, is very important to your success in this industry. Conversely, a negative attitude will stop you from experiencing the many benefits temping can offer. It is also worth noting that professionals, executives, and lawyers, will have an especially difficult time getting temp work if they show any bitterness or resentment to their "new" working arrangement or are too overanxious about getting a full-time job. It's like that old story about getting a loan: If you really don't need the money, a bank just loves to lend it to you. It was also found in a study of locum tenens physicians at one service, that the doctors who are most successful at it are the ones who are doing it for the fun and the experience. It all boils down to attitude. So, let's just amend that formula a bit:

Flexibility + Good Attitude = Success

And there's no reason why you shouldn't have a good attitude about temping. You've seen in this book that it is a very respectable thing to do; there's no negative image or stigma attached to temping whatsoever—from the mail room all the way up to the boardroom. The assignments will come, the full-time job offers will come, and the opportunities will come, as long as you keep your attitude right.

So temp. Have a good time doing it. Find a full-time job through it or make it a career. It's up to you. Good luck.

Index

ARCO is the leading publisher of study guides for every kind of test. Look for these titles at your favorite bookstore.

HIGH SCHOOL ENTRANCE

Catholic High School Entrance Examinations
High School Entrance Exams
New York City Specialized High School Entrance
    Examinations

COLLEGE ENTRANCE

ACT: American College Testing Program
ACT English Workbook
ACT Math Workbook
Advanced Placement Examinations in Mathematics: Calculus
    AB and Calculus BC
AP American History
AP Biology
AP Chemistry
AP English Literature and Composition
AP European History
AP United States Government and Politics
Preparation for the CLEP: College-Level Examination Program
Preparation for the SAT and PSAT
SAT Math Workbook
SAT Verbal Workbook

Continued...

SAT II Math: Level IC • Level IIC
SAT II Writing
TOEFL: Test of English as a Foreign Language
TOEFL Grammar Workbook
TOEFL Reading and Vocabulary Workbook
TOEFL Skills for Top Scores

CRAM COURSES

ACT Cram Course
GMAT Cram Course
GRE Cram Course
LSAT Cram Course
SAT Cram Course

SUPERCOURSES

ACT SuperCourse
GMAT SuperCourse
GRE SuperCourse
LSAT SuperCourse
SAT SuperCourse
SAT II: Subject Tests SuperCourse
MCAT SuperCourse
TOEFL SuperCourse

GRADUATE AND PROFESSIONAL SCHOOL ENTRANCE

Allied Health Professions
GMAT: Graduate Management Admission Test
Graduate Record Examination in Biology
Graduate Record Examination in Psychology
GRE: Graduate Record Examination

Continued...

GRE • GMAT Math Review
GRE • LSAT Logic Workbook
LSAT: Law School Admission Test
MAT: Miller Analogies Test
MCAT Sample Exams: Medical College Admission Test
Nursing School Entrance Examinations
PCAT: Pharmacy College Admission Test

MILITARY TESTS

ASVAB Basics
ASVAB en Español
Military Flight Aptitude Tests
Officer Candidate Tests
Practice for Air Force Placement Tests
Practice for the Armed Forces Test—ASVAB
Practice for Army Placement Tests

ADULT EDUCATION

GED: High School Equivalency Examination
GED en Español
GED Mathematics Workbook
GED Writing Skills Workbook
The Complete Guide to Becoming a U.S. Citizen

PROFESSIONAL CERTIFICATION AND LICENSING

The AICPA's Uniform CPA Exam
Automobile Technician Certification Tests
CBEST: California Basic Educational Skills Test
Counselor
Math Review for Real Estate License Examinations

Continued...

NTE / Praxis II
PPST / Praxis I
Real Estate License Examinations
Real Estate Licensing SuperCourse
Refrigeration License Examinations
Registered Representative / Stockbroker: Series 7 Exam
Teacher Certification Tests
Truck Driver's Guide to Commercial Driver Licensing

CIVIL SERVICE

Accountant / Auditor
ACWA: Administrative Careers With America
Air Traffic Controller
American Foreign Service Officer
Beginning Clerical Worker
Bookkeeper / Account Clerk
Building Custodian / Building Superintendent / Custodian
     Engineer
Bus Operator / Conductor
Case Worker
Civil Service Administrative Tests
Civil Service Arithmetic and Vocabulary
Civil Service Handbook
Civil Service Tests for Basic Skills Jobs
Clerical Exams Handbook
Correction Officer
Correction Officer Promotion Tests
Court Officer / Senior Court Officer / Court Clerk
Electrician / Electrician's Helper
Emergency Dispatcher / 911 Operator
File Clerk / General Clerk
Fire Department Lieutenant / Captain / Battalion Chief
Firefighter
General Test Practice for 101 U.S. Jobs

Continued...

Law Enforcement Exams Handbook
Mail Handler / Mail Processor
Maintenance Worker / Mechanical Maintainer
Police Officer
Police Sergeant / Lieutenant / Captain
Postal Exams Handbook
Post Office Clerk and Carrier
Practice for Clerical, Typing, and Stenographic Tests
Principal Administrative Associate / Administrative Assistant
Probation Officer / Parole Officer
Railroad Clerk
Railroad Porter / Cleaner
Sanitation Worker
Special Agent / Treasury Enforcement Agent
State Trooper / Highway Patrol Officer / State Traffic Officer
Storekeeper / Stock Handler
Track Worker
Traffic Enforcement Agent

AVAILABLE AT BOOKSTORES EVERYWHERE

MACMILLAN • USA